VOLUME 2
OUTER SPACE

The Moon

VOLUME 2
OUTER SPACE

The Moon

Robert Hitt, Jr.

Grolier Educational

SHERMAN TURNPIKE, DANBURY, CONNECTICUT 06816

WAUPACA AREA PUBLIC LIBRARY
107 South Main Street
Waupaca, WI 54981

Published 1998 by
Grolier Educational
Danbury, Connecticut 06816

Michael Friedman Publishing Group, Inc.
Editors: Susan Lauzau, Nathaniel Marunas,
and Celeste Sollod
Art Director: Jeff Batzli
Designers: Elan Studio, Devorah Wolf,
and Lynne Yeamans
Photography Editors: Karen Barr and Deidra Gorgos
Illustration Art Direction: Deidra Gorgos

Copyright © 1998 by
Michael Friedman Publishing Group, Inc.
Published for the school and library market exclusively
by Grolier Educational 1998

All rights in this book are reserved. No part of this book may be used or reproduced in any manner whatsoever or transmitted in any form or by any means, electronic or mechanical, including photocopying, recording, or any information storage and retrieval system, without written permission from the copyright owner except in the case of brief quotations embodied in critical articles and reviews. For information, address the publisher: Grolier Educational, Danbury, Connecticut 06816.

Published by arrangement with
Michael Friedman Publishing Group, Inc.
15 West 26th Street
New York, NY 10010

Library of Congress Cataloging in Publication Data

Outer space.
    p. cm.
    Includes bibliographical references and index.
    Contents: v. 1. The sun's family — v. 2. The moon — v. 3. The inner planets — v. 4. The outer planets — v. 5. The night sky — v. 6. Stars and galaxies — v. 7. Astronomy — v. 8. Space travel - v. 9. Space Shuttle — v. 10. Astronauts and cosmonauts — v. 11. Space stations — v. 12. Satellites and probes.
    ISBN 0-7172-9179-0 (set)
    1. Astronomy—Juvenile literature. 2. Outer space—Juvenile literature. 3. Astronautics—Juvenile literature. [1. Astronomy. 2. Outer space. 3. Astronautics.] I. Grolier Educational (Firm)
QB46.O826 1998
520–DC21   97-49010

First Edition
Printed in England

Photo Credits

Front jacket photography: UCO/Lick Observatory
Back jacket photography: NASA

Art Resource: p. 41

Lloyd Birmingham: Illustrations: pp. 10, 12, 13, 15, 21, 23 both, 25, 33, 45

Courtesy Celestron International: p. 8

Greg Harris: Illustrations: pp. 34–35, 37

Itar-Tass Express: p. 5 top

NASA: pp. 5 bottom left, 7 bottom right, 11, 14, 17, 18, 28 bottom, 29 both, 30, 31, 34 left, 38 right, 42 right, 44, 46 bottom, 47, 49, 51

Tom Stack and Associates: JPL/TSADO: p. 1; NASA/JPL/TSADO: p. 16; NASA/TSADO: pp. 2, 5 bottom right, 52–53; ©Mike O'Brine: p. 26; ©Wendy Shatil & Bob Rozinski: pp. 6–7

©UC Regents UCO/Lick Observatory: pp. 19, 22 all photographs in collage, 28 top, 32, 36 both, 38 left, 39, 40, 42 left

UPI/Corbis-Bettmann: p. 46 top, 48

CONTENTS

Introduction	6
How the Moon Was Formed	9
It Takes Two to Orbit	17
The Phases of the Moon	18
Lunar Eclipses	24
The Moon's Varied Terrain	28
Mapping the Moon	41
The Apollo Expeditions	43
Conclusion	52
Glossary	54
Set Index	58

INTRODUCTION

The Moon is Earth's closest celestial neighbor. It orbits Earth fewer than a quarter of a million miles (400,000km) away and is the second-brightest object in the sky after the Sun. Throughout history this mysterious glowing orb has fascinated people as it has traveled through the sky.

Myths and legends about the Moon, some of which are still told today, were created by civilizations around the world. Some ancient observers regarded it as a god that ruled the night, just as the Sun ruled the day. To early Greek and Roman astronomers the Moon was one of the seven magic celestial objects that moved (the others were the Sun and the five visible planets, Venus, Mercury, Mars, Jupiter, and Saturn) **(Vol. 5, pp. 13–14)**. As a timepiece the Moon was indispensable to early agricultural efforts; farmers learned to rely on its phases to time the planting and harvesting of crops. And on a more contemporary note, who hasn't heard of the Man in the Moon, or that the Moon is made of cheese? Such stories about the Moon abound, adding to its allure.

At first many people believed that the Moon was a world like Earth, inhabited by living beings. There were even some fanciful tales written describing Moon creatures with fur who spoke in musical notes. Later it was discovered that the Moon is very different from Earth and is unable to support any known life forms.

Over time some of the Moon's mysteries have been solved, but many more remain. For instance, there is still much debate over how the Moon was

▼ This close-up view of the lunar surface was taken by the astronauts of Apollo 8 as they orbited the Moon.

INTRODUCTION

This photograph of the Full Moon shows major craters and lunar "seas," or maria, which appear as dark areas.

formed. Even with the lunar samples collected by the Apollo missions **(pp. 43–51)** at their disposal, scientists are not certain of the origin of the Moon. The discovery of frozen water on the Moon in the early 1990s—strange because the lack of air pressure on the Moon would usually mean the water would evaporate into space—demonstrates that our satellite still holds many secrets **(p. 38)**. We have only explored a small part of its surface, and there remain many opportunities for further exploration. In this book we will examine the history of the observation of the Moon, discover why it looks the way it does, and find out what we have learned as a result of the visits that humans or machines have made to its surface.

INTRODUCTION

HOW THE MOON WAS FORMED

It seems strange that in an age when scientists are improving our understanding of the atom, cloning living animals, and landing remote-controlled explorers on Mars **(Vol. 3, pp. 50–51)**, we have not been able to explain how Earth's Moon formed. Over the centuries several theories have been put forward, and in the twentieth century scientists have examined more than 800 pounds (363kg) of lunar rocks, but the Moon's exact origin remains unknown.

The birth of the Moon probably occurred about the same time as the formation of the solar system. Current scientific thinking suggests that the Sun and planets were all formed in a giant **nebula** (a huge cloud of space dust and gas) **(Vol. 1, pp. 8–11)**. At the center of the nebula a large ball of gas coalesced and became the Sun, and the smaller pockets of gas circling it became the planets. As the nebula began to collapse and spin, small eddies, or currents, circling the forming planets began to shape into moons. This theory suggests that all the planets and moons are formed out of the same basic material. But close examination of some of the planets and their moons has shown this to be untrue. In the case of Earth's Moon, for instance, there are chemical differences between the Moon and Earth that require another explanation for the satellite's development. In addition, many of the planets are different from each other, and their moons also might have differences in what they are made of.

One thing that seems certain is that all the objects in the solar system are about the same age. The Sun possibly began as a ball of gases approximately five billion years ago, with the planets and their moons developing a few million years later. Based on the study of some of Earth's oldest known rocks and the Moon rocks retrieved by project Apollo, the Earth and Moon both appear to be between 3.3 to 4.6 billion years old. Future space missions to other planets and their moons might confirm this as the age of Earth's solar system.

The Fission Model

Another theory about the Moon's formation is the so-called **fission model**. Developed in 1879 by George Darwin (1845–1912), son of the famous naturalist Charles Darwin, the fission model suggests that the Earth and Moon were originally one mass, and the Moon was thrown off by the spinning of Earth. In order for this to have occurred, Earth would have to have been in a somewhat molten state, spinning much faster than it is today. This fast spin would have placed the outer layers of Earth in a condition known as **unbalanced equilibrium**; this means the Earth's gravity would not be able to keep hold of these outer layers. In this unstable condition the fast-spinning

▲ This is an illustration of the fission model of the Moon's origin. In the box on the left a fast-spinning Earth develops a bulge at the equator; in the box on the right the bulge has separated from the planet and is settling into orbit as the Moon.

Earth would appear somewhat flattened at its poles, and Earth's **mantle (see sidebar)** near the equator would experience a **tidal effect** (a bulge) caused by the **centrifugal force (Vol. 1, p. 14)** generated by the spin. This tide of planetary material would increase with the pull of the Sun's gravity, and eventually a large portion of this tidal bulge might be thrown into space. The material might then settle into a stable orbit near Earth.

The fission model is somewhat supported by a comparison of the **density** of Earth's mantle rocks with that of Moon rocks, which reveals some similarities. It has been suggested that the material for the Moon might have come from the basin now occupied by the largest ocean on Earth, the Pacific Ocean. This does not seem possible, however, because a chunk of Earth's mantle the size of the Pacific Ocean basin would not be large enough to form the Moon.

The fission model has been dealt some serious blows over time. For example, the Apollo mission returned lunar samples in

EARTH'S MANTLE

The mantle is the layer between the crust and the core of Earth, and extends nearly 1,800 miles (2,896km) toward the center of the planet. **(Vol. 3, p. 32)**

HOW THE MOON WAS FORMED

the 1960s and 1970s that were very different in chemical composition from the rocks lining Earth's ocean basins, which are part of Earth's mantle. Another problem with the fission model involves the rotational speed (speed at which the Earth turns) of Earth at the time of the Moon's formation. Calculations show that Earth would have to have been rotating once every 2.5 hours (it takes 24 hours now) in order to have thrown off the material that formed the Moon. Scientists have a couple of theories to explain how Earth could ever have spun that quickly.

One possibility involves the formation of the Earth's **core** (or center) billions of years ago. When the relatively dense iron sank to the center of Earth and became the core, it increased the rotational speed of the planet (in much the same way figure skaters speed up their spin by bringing their arms inward). Another possible explanation is that Earth's rotational speed may have been accelerated by impacts of comets, asteroids, or meteorites. However, computer simulations show that for every impact that would have increased the rotational speed (by hitting it in the same direction it was rotating), there would have been an equal number of impacts decreasing the speed.

▶ This photograph of the lunar surface, taken by the crew of Apollo 12 and showing the Sea of Storms, has a good view of the regolith, the loose, rocky stratum that covers the Moon.

Another problem with the fission model involves the Moon's orbit. If the Moon did get thrown off Earth's mantle, it would be orbiting in alignment with Earth's **equatorial plane**. This is an imaginary flat surface that bisects the Earth at the equator. In fact, the Moon's orbit tilt fluctuates between 18.5 degrees and 28.5 degrees off the Earth's equatorial plane. And yet another problem involves the **period** (the amount of time it takes to complete one pass around the Earth) of the Moon's orbit. In order for the Moon to be at its current distance and travel at its current orbit speed, it would have to have been thrown from the Earth only 1.2 million years ago. This is impossible, however, because the Earth had cooled and was solid by then (a fact that is revealed through the study of the Earth's geological record).

HOW THE MOON WAS FORMED

11

The Capture Model

The **capture model** of the Moon's formation suggests that Earth's **gravitational force** (an attraction that exists between all solid objects in proportion to their size and density) "captured" the fully formed Moon as it passed by. This theory might explain the differences in the chemical composition of Earth and the Moon, which would have formed in different parts of the solar system. It also might explain why the Moon is moving away from Earth. For the capture model to make sense, the Moon would have to have passed very close to Earth at the time of its capture. Around 1.2 billion years ago the Moon would have been close enough—about 11,200 miles (18,000km) away—to be captured. The problem with this is that the current orbit position of the Moon indicates that the Moon was captured more than 5 billion years ago, while the study of the Moon's rocks suggests that it is nowhere near that old.

The main problem with the capture model, however, is that Earth more than likely would have either collided with an object that came so close or would have flung it gravitationally (in a sort of slingshot effect) out of the neighborhood, or even out of the solar system. It would also be exceedingly unlikely for the orbits of the Moon and Earth to coincide in the precise way necessary to facilitate capture.

▼ This is an illustration of the capture model of the Moon's origin. In the box on the left the fully formed Moon travels near Earth as it moves through space; in the box on the right Earth's gravity has "captured" the passing Moon in a stable orbit.

HOW THE MOON WAS FORMED

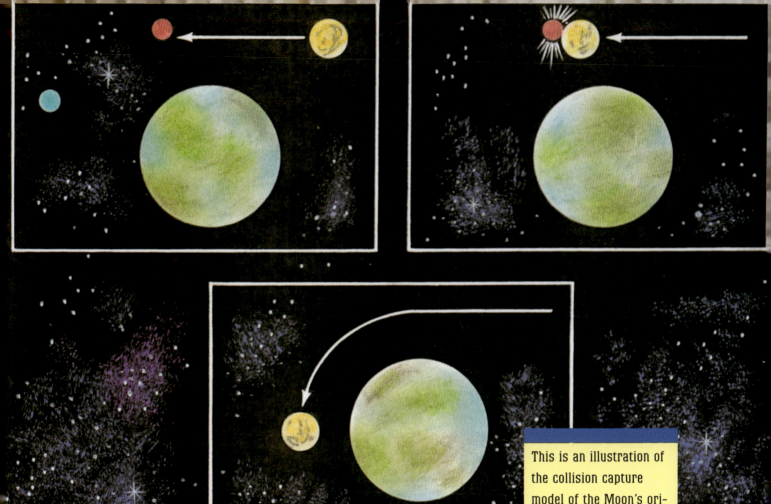

This is an illustration of the collision capture model of the Moon's origin. In the box on the top left the fully formed Moon travels near Earth, which is surrounded by a few small moons; in the box on the top right the Moon collides with these small satellites and absorbs their mass, which causes it to slow down; in the bottom box the slowed Moon has been "captured" in orbit by Earth's gravity.

Collision Capture Model

The **collision capture model** suggests that the capture model might work if Earth once had a family of smaller moons orbiting it. Then a larger moon could have passed into Earth's orbit and crashed into some, or all, of these smaller moons. As these smaller moons collided with the incoming object, the speed of that object would decrease, allowing capture by Earth's gravity. This also might account for the formation of **lunar maria** and **lava flows (pp. 30–32)**, which could have formed in the heat generated during these collisions. The main problem with this theory is there is no proof that Earth ever had several smaller moons.

The Double Planet Model

Earth and the Moon are often considered a **double planet system** (in which the gravitational forces of two relatively close

HOW THE MOON WAS FORMED

BARYCENTER

Earth's mass is eighty-one times greater than the mass of the Moon. The common center of mass (or balance point) between the two bodies is a point located 1,000 miles (1,609km) below Earth's crust. The Moon orbits around the Earth relative to this point, not to the center of the Earth. It is important to note that when there are two masses that are within the attraction of the other's gravity, the center of gravity will be located closer to the center of the larger mass.

celestial objects of similar size interact). Our Moon is almost one-fourth the size of Earth, and both objects orbit around a common **center of mass**, referred to as a **barycenter (see sidebar)**. The only other example of this phenomenon in our solar system is Pluto and its moon Chiron.

The **double planet model** suggests the Moon and Earth formed almost five billion years ago in a cloud of dust and gas. In its early development stages Earth formed a ring of material around its equator as it slowly began to spin. This material eventually came together to form our Moon. This implies

Apollo 12 astronaut Charles Conrad, Jr., unloads equipment in preparation for exploring the lunar surface.

that the Moon is made of planetary "leftovers." This model explains some of the chemical similarities between Earth and the Moon, but it does not explain why there are also chemical dissimilarities. The double planet model also does not explain why the Earth's iron core is large relative to the core of the Moon. If both bodies formed out of the same cloud of gas and dust, they would be expected to have iron cores of similar sizes with respect to their overall sizes. Instead, the Moon's iron core is estimated to be only 450 miles (730km) in diameter (out of 2,200 miles [3,500km] total diameter), while the Earth's core is estimated to be more than 4,000 miles (6,500km) in diameter (out of 8,000 miles [12,750km] total).

▼ This is an illustration of the giant impact model of the Moon's origin, showing a Mars-sized object colliding with Earth; part of the huge object will sink into the core of the planet, while some of the object, mixed with material from Earth, will be launched into orbit.

The Giant Impact Model

In the early history of the solar system there were many large space rocks and planet-size chunks of matter spinning through space, providing ample opportunity for large-scale collisions. A close examination of the other planets and their moons reveals numerous craters and scars from such collisions. The tilt of Uranus is possibly the result of a gigantic impact with a space neighbor. Over time the planets and their moons have swept the solar system clean of much of its former space debris. Today there are only a few million objects remaining, drifting around the Sun, and collisions do not happen very often.

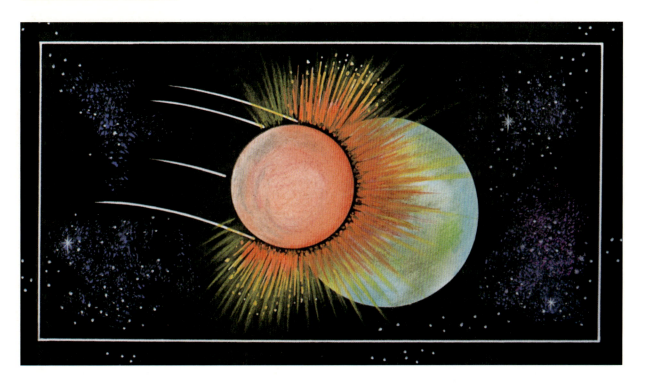

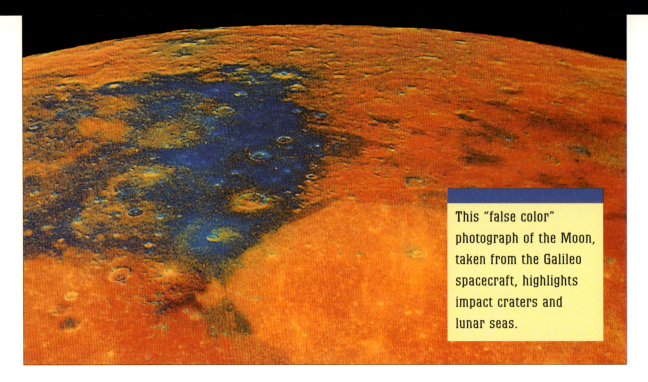

This "false color" photograph of the Moon, taken from the Galileo spacecraft, highlights impact craters and lunar seas.

A more recent theory of the Moon's origin than the ones above proposes that Earth may have collided with just such a planet-size object. This is known as the **giant impact model**. First proposed in 1946 by Harvard geologist Reginald Daly (1871–1957), this model suggests that the early solar system contained many small to planet-size objects flying around the Sun. The theory proposes that one of the larger of these objects collided with Earth, throwing some of its own mass and Earth's mass into orbit. In this giant impact model the object of the collision is estimated to have been about 4,000 miles (6,436km) in diameter, or about the size of the planet Mars. Most of the object's mass would have sunk to the center of Earth, which at the time was a huge ball of molten material covered with a thin crust, but a smaller portion of the less dense material would have mixed with Earth's material and would have been launched into orbit. Some of the material that was launched into space would collect together due to gravity and form the Moon. This would explain why the Moon does not have a large iron core.

The giant impact model also explains some of the similarities and dissimilarities in the chemistry of Earth and the Moon. Such a massive collision would have created great heat in the smaller mass of the Moon, evaporating any water and leaving the Moon dry. An impact just off-center from Earth's axis of rotation would also explain why our planet rotates faster than expected. If the collision occurred in the same direction as the spin of the Earth, it would increase the rotation speed. (Likewise, an impact off-center in the opposite direction of the spin of the Earth would have slowed the rotation speed.) Many scientists believe that Earth, in its early history, rotated more slowly than it does now. In addition, the giant impact model might explain why the orbit of the Moon is tilted off the equatorial plane. The problem with this theory of the Moon's origins, as with the other theories, is that there is no positive proof that any of them is correct.

IT TAKES TWO TO ORBIT

Although the Moon is orbiting Earth, it is also currently moving away from the planet. The gravitational pull between Earth and the Moon produces what is called **tidal friction** (a braking force). This tidal friction transfers some of Earth's rotational energy to the Moon. As a result the Moon's orbital speed is increasing as the Earth's rotational speed is decreasing, and the Moon is moving away from Earth at the rate of several inches per year. Do not worry about the Moon leaving Earth, though—the gravity between the two will eventually cause the Moon and Earth to reach **equilibrium**.

When equilibrium occurs, the Moon will be orbiting at the same rate that the Earth is rotating, about once every 47 days. It is estimated that when this occurs, the Moon will be located at a distance of more than 350,000 miles (560,000km) from Earth. This is not expected to happen for many billions of years, which may exceed the lifespan of the solar system. If the Earth and Moon ever do reach equilibrium, the effects of the tidal friction will be reversed: the Earth will start pulling the Moon back toward it and begin to reabsorb energy from the Moon's orbital rotation. This will cause Earth's rotational speed to increase as the Moon's orbital speed decreases. There is no need to be concerned about the Moon crashing into Earth, though: astronomers suggest there is a limit **(see sidebar on Roche's Limit)** to how close the Moon can

ROCHE'S LIMIT

Edouard Roche (1820–1883), a French mathematician, discovered a mathematical relationship describing how close a moon and its **primary** (the planet around which it orbits) can orbit in equilibrium. This limit depends on the density of the two bodies in orbit. For the Moon, which has a density that is lower than that of Earth, the **Roche limit** would be 2.9 Earth radiuses, or approximately 12,000 miles (19,300km).

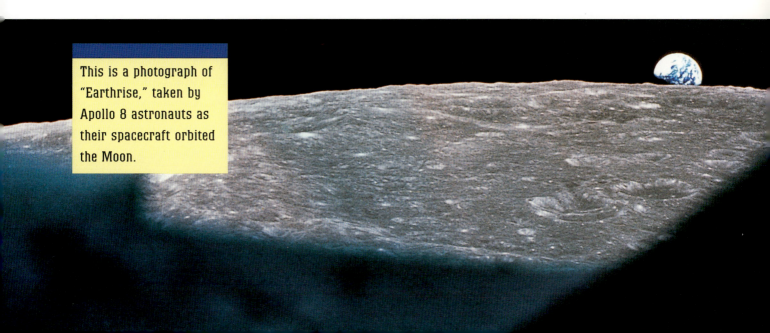

This is a photograph of "Earthrise," taken by Apollo 8 astronauts as their spacecraft orbited the Moon.

◀ This photograph of the Full Moon was taken by the crew of Apollo 16 as they were on their way back to Earth. This view shows more of the eastern edge of the Moon than is visible from Earth.

come to Earth before Earth's gravity will stress the Moon and possibly break it into many small pieces. If that were to happen, Earth would have a ring around it as Saturn does.

If the Moon ever came close enough to Earth to be pulled apart, Earth's surface would also be destroyed by the tremendous gravitational pull of the Moon. In any event, this will not happen any time soon. In fact, most astronomers estimate it would take over ten billion years. By then our Sun will have made other changes in the solar system **(Vol. 6, pp. 23–26)**.

This transfer of energy between Earth and the Moon is also affecting the rotational speed of Earth. Earth is currently slowing down, and our days are getting longer. It is estimated that the daily rotational rate of Earth is increasing by 2/10,000,000 of a second each day. Do not reset your alarm clock, though—at this rate the day will be only one second longer in 100,000 years.

THE PHASES OF THE MOON

As the Moon orbits Earth, its shape appears to change every day. This puzzled early civilizations, some of which developed ideas to explain the phenomenon. To the earliest civilizations the Moon's phases were used as a means of recording the passage of time and were the basis for the first calendars. These calendars were not terribly accurate and were not synchronized with the seasons. Eventually the **Moon-phase**, or lunar, calendars were replaced with **solar calendars**, based on our yearly revolution around the Sun, which recognized seasonal changes. Today we know that the Moon reflects sunlight, and that it seems to change shape because different parts of the Moon's surface are illuminated (by the Sun) as it orbits Earth.

▲ These two photographs illustrate the process of libration, which enables Earthbound viewers to see roughly 59 percent of the Moon's surface at different times. Note the difference on the eastern, or right, edge of each photograph.

These changes in illumination are called **phases**.

To understand the motions of the Moon and Earth, it is best to understand a few simple facts about our planet and its satellite. First, Earth is in orbit around the Sun, which means that each day Earth travels approximately 2,000,000 miles (3,200,000km) in its orbit path. Second, the Moon is revolving around Earth and completes one orbit around the planet every 27.3 days. This period is called a **sidereal month**.

There are also several things about the Moon's orbit that should be understood. The Moon's orbit is not a perfect circle; instead, it is an **ellipse (Vol. 5, pp. 16–17)**. Also, the Moon appears to move across the sky from east to west, but this is not the true motion of the Moon around Earth. The Moon is actually orbiting our planet in an easterly motion. The illusion occurs because Earth is rotating faster than the Moon orbits our planet. The Moon is constantly losing ground and appears to move

THE DARK SIDE OF THE MOON?

As the Moon orbits Earth we only get to see one side of its surface. There is always a side that points away from our view. It is often called the dark side of the Moon, but this is an inaccurate term because there is no side of the Moon that is always dark.

In the extreme polar regions of the Moon there are several deep craters that never receive sunlight inside their walled edges. These areas are the only places on the Moon that truly always are dark.

THE PHASES OF THE MOON

west to set. You can observe this phenomenon if you line up the Moon with a star in the sky and look for the star on the next night at the same time. The Moon will have moved eastward through the star field by about 13°. This eastward motion is what causes the Moon to rise about fifty minutes later each day. One final fact about the Moon is that its orbital speed is constantly changing due to the shape of its orbit and the pull of the Earth's and the Sun's gravity **(pp. 22–24)**.

Moon Phases

Now let us consider the entire 360° orbit of the Moon and show how the Moon's apparent shape changes over the course of one lunar orbit. The diagram on page 21 does not show the movement of Earth in its orbit.

Position 1: The Moon is between Earth and the Sun. The back of the Moon is fully illuminated, and the side facing Earth is dark. This is called the **New Moon**.

Position 2: The Moon has moved 45° (from the Sun) to the east around Earth and now shows a small sunlit edge; this is called a **Crescent Moon**. More specifically, this is called the **Waxing** ("getting larger") **Crescent Moon**, and it is visible in the western sky after sunset for several days after the New Moon.

Position 3: Approximately seven days after the New Moon the Moon has moved 90° from the Sun and is one-quarter of the way around Earth. It appears to be half-illuminated. This is not called a half moon; instead, it is called the **First Quarter Moon**. From Earth an observer can actually only see one-quarter of the Moon's surface; the other illuminated quarter is on the far side of the Moon. The eastern half of the Moon appears dark in this position. The First Quarter Moon can be observed high in the southern sky near your local **meridian** (an imaginary line running north-to-south and passing through a point directly overhead) at sunset.

Position 4: The Moon is approximately 135° away from the Sun and appears to be three-quarters illuminated. This is called the **Waxing Gibbous Moon** ("gibbous" is Latin for "more than half"). It appears in the eastern sky just before sunset.

Position 5: The Moon is now opposite the Sun (180° away) on the far side of Earth and will rise at sunset. It now appears to be fully illuminated and is called the **Full Moon**. At this time the back of the Moon is completely dark.

KEEPING TRACK OF THE LUNATIONS

A lunation is the time from one New Moon to the next. The numbering of lunations started on the Full Moon of January 17, 1923. Most astronomical almanacs include lunation numbers, along with dates of lunar phases and the age of the Moon (counted in days) at the start of each lunation. For example, the New Moon of December 29, 1997, was the start of lunation number 928, at which time the Moon was 0 days old. The full Moon of January 12, 1998, was also lunation number 928, but the Moon was 14 days old.

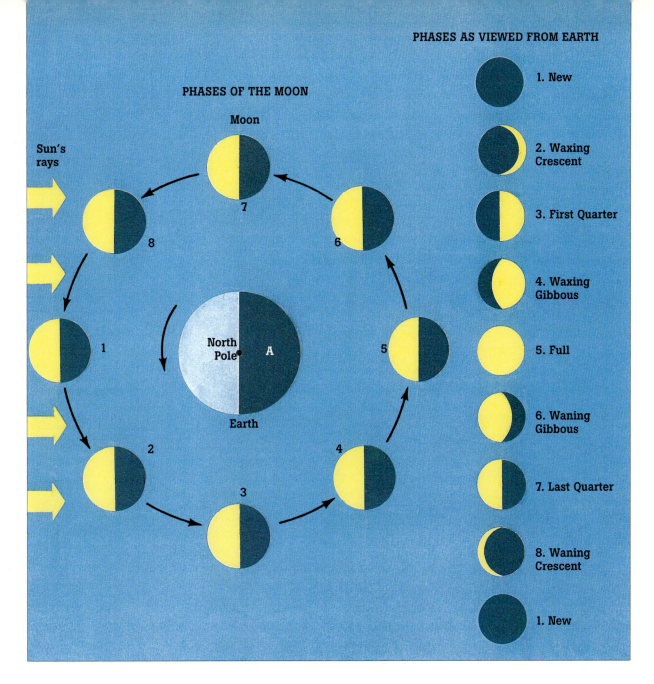

Position 6: The Moon has moved 225° from the Sun, and the dark edge of the Moon is visible again. This time it is on the opposite side, the eastern edge, of the lunar disk that faces Earth. This is called the **Waning** ("getting smaller") **Gibbous Moon**. It rises after sunset.

Position 7: The Moon is now three-quarters of the way around Earth (270° from the Sun) and once again appears to be half-illuminated. This is called the **Last Quarter Moon**. The western half of the Moon now appears dark.

Position 8: Now at 315° degrees away from where it started, the Moon is almost back to its position between Earth and the Sun. This is called the **Waning Crescent Moon** and is visible in the early-morning sky before sunrise. Soon the Moon will be back to Position 1 and will again be in the New Moon phase. The total cycle from one New Moon, or full moon, to the next is called a **lunar** or **synodic month**, or a **lunation**, and takes 29.5 days.

THE PHASES OF THE MOON

The Moon Catches Up

Why does it take the Moon 27.32 days to orbit our planet but 29.5 days from one New Moon to the next? The reason for this difference is that Earth is moving in its orbit around the Sun at the same time the Moon is orbiting around Earth. This means it takes additional time for the Moon to line up with the Sun and Earth for the next New Moon. In other words, the Moon must orbit an additional amount to compensate for Earth's own orbit. It takes the Moon about two days to catch up.

Synchronous Rotation

As you can see from the Moon-phase diagrams in this book, all sides of the Moon do get sunlight during some part of the Moon's orbit.

It is also true, however, that observers on Earth only get to see one side of the Moon. Many people think this is because it does not rotate. This is incorrect: the Moon does rotate on its axis, but it rotates in exactly the same amount of time that it takes to orbit Earth and complete its cycle of phases. This is known as **synchronous rotation**. The best way to

◄ These photographs show the phases of the Moon (not including, of course, the New Moon): Waxing Crescent, First Quarter, Waxing Gibbous, Full, Waning Gibbous, Second Quarter, Waning Crescent.

THE PHASES OF THE MOON

demonstrate the effect of this phenomenon is to consider the diagrams below.

The boxes on this page are "overhead" views of the Moon's orbit. From this perspective the Moon orbits in a counterclockwise direction. At top the Moon does not rotate on its axis as it orbits Earth. The surface is marked with an X as a reference point. In position 1 X is facing Earth and is visible. Notice that in position 2 the X is visible on the left edge of the Moon, but in position 3 the X is not visible because it is on the far side of the Moon. If the Moon did not rotate, observers on Earth would be able to see what was on the back of the Moon.

In fact, the Moon spins on its axis as illustrated in the bottom box. X will always be visible from Earth no matter where the Moon is in its orbit. This is why observers on Earth never get to see the back of the Moon. This motion can also be demonstrated by having someone sit in a chair in the middle of the

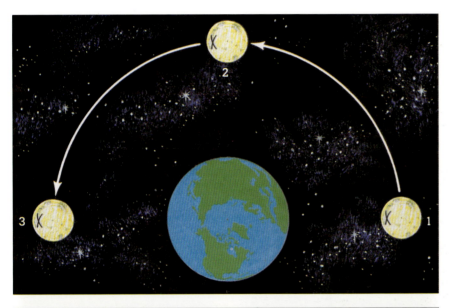

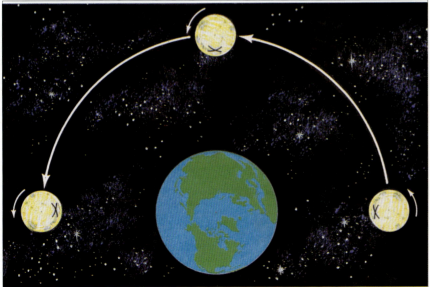

◀

These illustrations show the effect of synchronous rotation. As shown in the top box, if the Moon did not rotate as it orbited the planet, an observer on Earth would be able to see both sides of the Moon; because the Moon rotates on its axis at the same rate at which it orbits, however, Earthbound observers only ever see the "front" side, which is always turning to face the planet.

THE PHASES OF THE MOON

room. Walk around the chair, always keeping the front of your body toward the person in the chair. You will have to turn or rotate constantly in order to keep them from seeing the back of your head. You have just completed one orbit, as well as one rotation. You were in synchronous rotation with the seated person. Now walk around the person, keeping a fixed (i.e., not rotating) position by always facing one corner of the room or a picture on the wall. The person will be able to see your front and your back at different points in your orbit.

The Shape of the Moon's Orbit

In observing the phases of the Moon, it is important to remember that the orbit of the Moon is not a perfect circle around Earth. It is an egg-shaped, or **elliptical** orbit (an ellipse is a flattened circle). As the Moon orbits Earth, its speed is constantly changing, depending on how far it is from the Sun **(Vol. 5, pp. 16–17)**.

> ### THE BLUE MOON
>
> There is usually only one Full Moon and one New Moon each calendar month. Sometimes the Moon phases and the days of the month coincide in such a way that there are two Full Moons in one month. In order for this to happen, the first Full Moon must occur near the first of the month. Anytime there are two Full Moons in one month, the second Full Moon is called the **Blue Moon**. It does not look blue, but it is a rare occurrence (7 times every 19 years); hence the expression "once in a blue moon."

This causes the Moon to appear to rock back and forth slightly as it orbits, a phenomenon known as **libration**. This effect allows Earthbound observers to see more than half—actually about 59%—of the lunar surface.

LUNAR ECLIPSES

Unlike an eclipse of the Sun, which can be seen only by a few people along a narrow strip of Earth's surface, an eclipse of the Moon can be viewed by an entire hemisphere. During a full **eclipse** the full Moon passes through the Earth's shadow. Anyone who can see the Moon at the time of a lunar eclipse will see the event. An eclipse of the Moon can occur only at the time of Full Moon, when the Moon is located 180° from the Sun and is aligned at the proper angle to pass into the shadow of Earth. In two-dimensional diagrams of the Moon's orbit the Moon appears to line up in Earth's shadow once every 29.5 days, but Earth's shadow does not perfectly align with the Moon during each orbit. The Moon's orbit is tilted, which usually causes the Moon to miss Earth's shadow completely.

How the Moon's Orbit Affects Lunar Eclipses

The Moon's orbit is not aligned with the **ecliptic** (an imaginary line that extends from the Sun to Earth that is often referred to as the plane of the solar system) but is tilted 5°

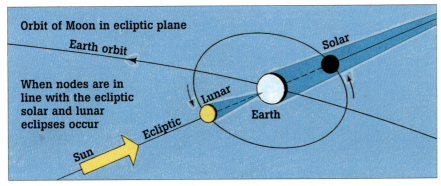
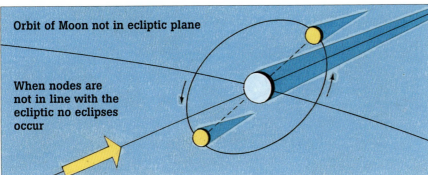
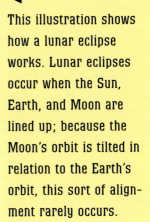

This illustration shows how a lunar eclipse works. Lunar eclipses occur when the Sun, Earth, and Moon are lined up; because the Moon's orbit is tilted in relation to the Earth's orbit, this sort of alignment rarely occurs.

from it. As the Moon orbits Earth, it crosses the ecliptic twice. These crossing points are called **nodes**: **ascending node** if the Moon is moving south to north of the ecliptic, and **descending node** if the Moon is moving north to south. In order for a lunar eclipse to occur, the Full Moon must be near one of these nodes in its orbit. To further complicate things, the nodes of the Moon's orbit are slowly moving westward along the ecliptic, and they complete one revolution every 18 years, 11 days. This period of time is called a **saros**. When the Moon's nodes have completed one saros, eclipses will occur on the same dates as they did 18 years ago (relative to variations in our calendar).

LUNAR ECLIPSE TERMINOLOGY

First contact = Moon enters penumbral shadow
Second contact = Moon enters umbra
Third contact = Beginning of total eclipse
Fourth contact = End of total eclipse
Fifth contact = Moon leaves umbra
Last contact = Moon leaves penumbral shadow

Earth's Shadow

Earth's shadow stretches more than 850,000 miles (1,367,650km) into outer space. The shadow is composed of two parts. The **umbra** is the darkest part of the shadow and is surrounded by a lighter shadow called the **penumbra**. If the Moon passes completely through Earth's umbra, the lunar eclipse will be **total**. If the Moon passes through only

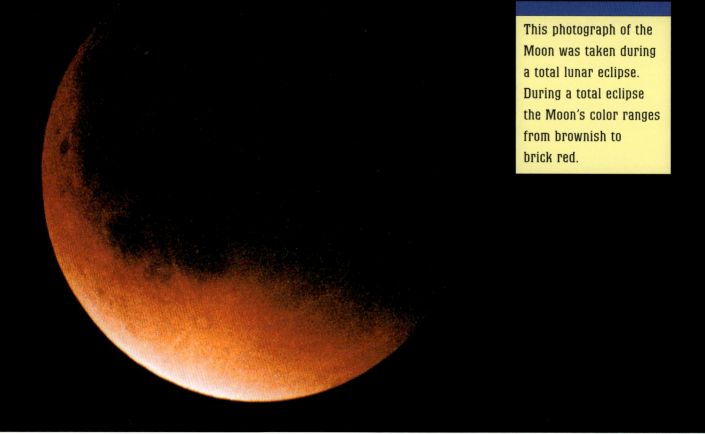

This photograph of the Moon was taken during a total lunar eclipse. During a total eclipse the Moon's color ranges from brownish to brick red.

part of the umbra, the lunar eclipse will be **partial**. During what is called a **penumbral eclipse** the Moon does not enter the umbra at all, instead just passing through the penumbra.

The unique feature of Earth's shadow is its color. It is not a black shadow. The atmosphere of Earth **refracts**, or bends, sunlight into the umbra and produces a reddish hue. Sunlight is a mixture of all colors in the visible spectrum, but only the longest **wavelengths of light (Vol. 7, pp. 16–17)**, the red ones, are refracted. The other colors in the spectrum are absorbed by the atmosphere of the planet. The color of a total lunar eclipse is determined by the condition of Earth's atmosphere. If there happens to be a lot of dust in the planet's atmosphere, perhaps from the eruption of a volcano, the Moon will appear very dark red and will almost completely disappear during a total eclipse, even if the eclipse occurs many months after the eruption. This phenomenon has happened only a few times in the last century. In 1963, for instance, Mount Agung on Bali in Indonesia erupted, spewing dust and gas into the atmosphere and darkening the lunar eclipse of December 30 of that year. In 1991 Mount Pinatubo in the Philippines ejected material that darkened the December 9, 1992, eclipse. If Earth's atmosphere is clear and free of pollutants, the Moon might appear only slightly orange during a lunar eclipse.

The Total Lunar Eclipse

In a total lunar eclipse there are dramatic effects in the night sky. As the Moon is dimmed by Earth's shadow, many faint stars can be seen near the **limb** (the outer edge of the visible disk of a celestial body) of the Moon. These stars are often blocked from view by the bright light of the Full Moon. Some of these stars can be viewed disappearing behind the Moon; this event is called an **occultation** and offers a chance to actually see the Moon moving slowly to the east in its orbit around Earth. There are also interesting observations to be made about the Moon's surface. During a total eclipse the soft color of Earth's shadow causes many lunar features to be illuminated in such a way that details are revealed that cannot normally be seen. It is also possible, by timing how long a certain lunar feature is in the umbra, to compute the span of Earth's shadow.

The width of Earth's shadow cone at the point of intersection with the Moon's orbit is approximately 5,700 miles (9,200km). Because the shadow is wider than the Moon, lunar eclipses last much longer than solar eclipses. From the time the Moon first enters Earth's shadow, the event can last more than five hours. Totality **(Vol. 1, pp. 34–35)** can last almost two hours if the Moon passes through the center of the shadow. If the Moon passes off-center, the time of totality will be shortened.

Famous Lunar Eclipses

Lunar eclipses have often affected the course of history. In 1453 the Turkish army defeated the Christian defenders of the city of Constantinople because of a total lunar eclipse. The phenomenon was perceived as a bad omen by the defenders, who lost their will to fight. In 1504 Christopher Columbus was stranded on the island of Jamaica. He could not get the local natives to help him repair his ship or supply him with food. Columbus knew there was going to be a total lunar eclipse on February 29 and used the event to his advantage. He informed the natives that there would be a great display of anger in the sky for the way he had been treated. When the eclipse occurred, the natives were frightened and came running to his aid, bringing food and supplies. Today we understand lunar eclipses and can predict them far into the future, but they are still a captivating and beautiful sight in the night sky.

TOTAL LUNAR ECLIPSES 1998–2010

January 21, 2000
July 16, 2000*
January 9, 2001*
May 16, 2003
November 9, 2003
May 4, 2004*
October 28, 2004
March 3, 2007
August 28, 2007
February 21, 2008
December 21, 2010

*Not visible in North America

THE MOON'S VARIED TERRAIN

The surface of the Moon appears the same today as it did almost four billion years ago because its surface features have not been subjected to such forces as weathering and erosion the way Earth's surface has. In addition, the Moon was totally untouched by humans until project **Apollo** landed astronauts on the surface in July 1969. By observing the Moon's surface through telescopes and by visiting it in person, we have learned several things about the Moon. On close examination of the lunar surface in the 1960s, for example, it was discovered that the Moon's "seas" **(p. 30)** are covered with a fine layer of broken surface rocks and dust called **regolith** (Greek for "rocky layer"). Apollo data confirmed depths of 6 to 30 feet (2–10m) of regolith at the landing sites. As it turns out, most of the Moon's surface is covered with regolith, which is made up of gray, fragmented **bedrock**, which is the solid rock below the surface. It has been said that the Moon's surface resembles powdered concrete.

Notable features of the Moon's surface include wrinkled ridges, domes, cliffs, **maria** (Latin for "seas"; the singular is **mare**), mountains, and craters. Lunar **wrinkles** look like crumpled skin and are visible in many places on the Moon. In Mare Serenitatis (Sea of Serenity) **(p. 32)** the ridges are visible crisscrossing the entire area. There is also a unique pattern of wrinkles in Mare Tranquillitatis (Sea of Tranquility), **(p. 32)** radiating out from the crater Lamont. Lunar **domes** appear as surface swellings where the lunar crust has been pushed up and deformed (by unknown forces). These generally occur in clusters and can only be observed in low-angle sunlight illumination. Some of these domes appear to be volcanoes with **summit pits** (craters at the top). They are found all over the lunar surface, and several are found inside lunar **craters (pp. 34–38)**. Cliffs are some of

◀ This telescopic view of the Moon's surface, near its southern limb, shows several craters, including Baco and Pitiscus (the largest two in the photograph).

▼ Taken from Apollo 12, this photograph shows a lunar mound near the landing site in the Sea of Storms.

MOON MYTHS

At first glance the Moon appears as a mosaic of light and dark areas. These areas are different shades due to the way sunlight is reflected off the surface of the Moon. Areas that are smooth appear dark, while the rough areas—that is, areas covered with craters and mountains—appear bright. It is these light and dark areas that suggest the face of the Man in the Moon. Other civilizations imagined numerous things as they viewed these light and dark regions. To the Chinese the Moon was a great toad, and in Germany there was a tale of an old man banished to the Moon for gathering firewood on a day set aside for rest. There is also a tale from India of why the wolf howls at the Moon. It seems the wolf was in love with a frog, and the only way the frog could escape the wolf's amorous advances was to jump to the Moon. Now at each Full Moon the wolf cries at the Moon, asking the frog to return to Earth. Countless other tales about the Moon exist in cultures around the world.

▲ The top photograph was taken by the crew of Apollo 10 from a distance of 60 miles (97km) above the lunar surface. Note the terracing of the crater sides and central mountain peak, a common feature of large craters. The bottom photograph is a view from Apollo 10 showing part of the crater Godin from a distance of 60 miles (97km). Godin is approximately 17 miles (27km) in diameter.

the most remarkable features on the lunar landscape. The most famous cliff is located near the eastern edge of Mare Nubium. This cliff is officially known as Rupes Recta but is more commonly called the Straight Wall. It is actually a giant **fault** (a place where the surface has collapsed) almost 70 miles (110km) long. The western portion of the fault is 1,000 feet (305m) below the eastern portion. In the right light the shadow gives the impression of a steep cliff, but the fault is actually a gradual slope. It can be observed easily with a small telescope during the First Quarter Moon. Other cliffs are found throughout the lunar landscape.

The Moon's most prominent features—visible even through a small pair of binoculars—are the seas, craters, and mountains.

THE MOON'S VARIED TERRAIN

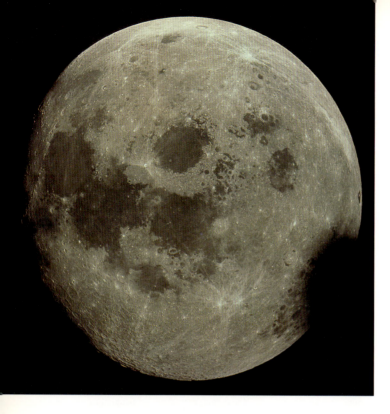

◀ Lunar features visible in this photograph include the Sea of Crisis, the Sea of Fertility, the Sea of Tranquillity, and the Sea of Serenity. This photograph was taken by the crew of Apollo 13 as they returned to Earth.

Seas

The seventeenth-century Italian scientist Galileo Galilei (1564–1642) **(Vol. 3, p. 10)** was not the first but was certainly one of the most famous observers of the Moon. In his earliest observations, around 1610, he noticed the Moon was smooth in places and rough in others. He also noticed many spots (craters) of different sizes and noted that the Moon was similar to Earth in that it had mountains and valleys. He made some attempts to measure the height of the lunar mountains and (incorrectly) concluded they were much taller than those found on Earth. Galileo noticed that most of the Moon's surface facing Earth was covered with smooth dark areas, which he named maria. The maria have never held water but are called seas because of their smooth sealike appearance.

Seas are the largest lunar features. On the side of the Moon facing Earth they cover more than 31 percent of the lunar surface. The maria are also the lowest points of elevation on the lunar surface, at roughly 2 miles (3km) below the surrounding moonscape. (Curiously, seas appear to have as much regolith **(p. 28)** as do the highland parts of the Moon.) Viewed though a small telescope, seas appear as large, flat stretches of water, so it is understandable that the earliest observers thought these were actual seas. They are still called oceans, seas, lakes, and marshes, but only as descriptive terminology, and not to suggest the existence of large bodies of water on the Moon.

The seas are divided into two categories, **circular** and **irregular**. Circular seas are usually bordered by mountains and craters, and appear well defined. The other type of sea is irregular, less defined, and often has boundaries that merge together with other lunar features. With the proper angle of sunlight, however, all maria display some unevenness and numerous craters. They are not as smooth as early observers thought. Nonetheless, their relatively smooth surfaces have made them logical targets for many remote and manned lunar landings **(pp. 43–51)**.

The origin of the seas has been debated for years. Lunar samples brought back by Apollo 11 revealed that below the regolith,

THE MOON'S VARIED TERRAIN

the seas had extensive lava flows covered with debris typical of meteorite impacts. Analysis of lunar rocks returned by Apollo 15 also hints at **lava flows** and collapsed **lava tubes**. These lava tubes may have once been filled with hot lava and gases, but later collapsed and now appear as depressions, or **rills**. The study of the lunar samples taken at each Apollo site revealed that different seas have different ages.

Several theories about the formation of the lunar surface are supported by these discoveries. For instance, much of the lunar surface may have been created by great volcanic lava flows more than 3.9 billion years ago. Or the lunar surface may have been melted by the bombardment of meteorites and asteroids. For instance, a large impact could have formed what is now known as Mare Imbrium. The heat of the impact would have melted the lunar surface, cracked the crust, and made lava flow, creating the largest sea on the side of the Moon visible from Earth. Alternatively, intense cratering activity on a smaller scale may have caused additional areas of the lunar surface to reheat and form smooth, sealike features. What seems certain, though, is that sometime around 3.8 billion years ago the lava flows stopped, and the formation of seas ended. The lunar surface we see today is basically unchanged since then, except for the occasional new meteor crater.

The largest dark area on the Moon is known as Oceanus Procellarum (Ocean of Storms). It is known as an ocean because of its size: it covers more than 63,000 square miles

This view from the command module of Apollo 11 shows the lunar module Eagle returning from the Moon to dock with the command module. The dark area in the background is Smyth's Sea; Earth is visible above the lunar horizon.

▲ This is a close-up of the Sea of Serenity. The large crater near the center at the top is Posidonius. The deep shadowed crater to the lower left is Eudoxus.

located near the western edge of the Moon. This sea was possibly created by a gigantic impact that occurred as much as 3.9 billion years ago. Mare Imbrium and Mare Orientale are two of the oldest features on the Moon.

(104,000 sq km) and appears on the western edge of lunar maps. Procellarum is clearly marked on the western, northern, and southern borders, but its eastern border is indefinite. Some of the bright lunar rays **(pp. 35–36)** radiating from the crater Kepler are easily visible across the ocean's dark-gray surface. Oceanus Procellarum appears to make up the "mouth" of the Man in the Moon. Other seas that can be observed with the naked eye on the Earth-side of the Moon are Mare Imbrium, Mare Serenitatis, Mare Tranquillitatis, Mare Fecunditatis, and Mare Crisium.

Of special interest is the area of the landing site of Apollo 11, in the lower western edge of Mare Tranquillitatis. On the side of the Moon we do not see, the so-called dark side **(p. 19)**, there is a large sea named Mare Orientale (Eastern Sea). It is

LUNAR SEAS AND OCEANS: LATIN-ENGLISH TRANSLATIONS

The names given to the seas and oceans of the Moon reflect the beliefs held at the time they were observed, when it was generally thought that the Moon had an influence on such aspects of life as fertility and dreams.

Latin Name	English Translation
Mare Anguis	Serpent Sea
Mare Australe	Southern Sea
Mare Cognitum	Known Sea
Mare Crisium	Sea of Crisis
Mare Fecunditatis	Sea of Fertility
Mare Frigoris	Sea of Cold
Mare Humboldtianum	Humboldt's Sea
Mare Humorum	Sea of Moisture
Mare Imbrium	Sea of Rains
Mare Insularum	Sea of Isles
Mare Marginis	Border Sea
Mare Nectaris	Sea of Nectar
Mare Nubium	Sea of Clouds
Mare Orientale	Eastern Sea
Mare Serenitatis	Sea of Serenity
Mare Smythii	Smyth's Sea
Mare Spumans	Foaming Sea
Mare Tranquillitatis	Sea of Tranquility
Mare Undarum	Sea of Waves
Mare Vaporum	Sea of Vapors
Oceanus Procellarum	Ocean of Storms

THE MOON'S VARIED TERRAIN

LUNAR MAPS

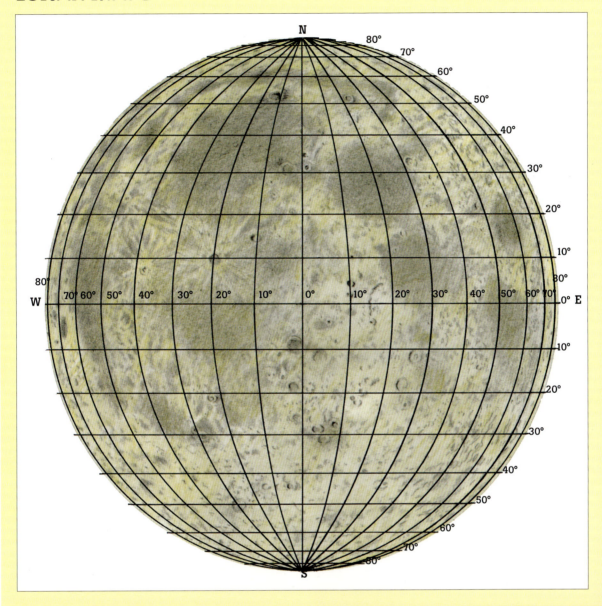

Some maps show the Moon upside-down, as it appears when viewed through an astronomy telescope, but in 1961 the International Astronomical Union (IAU) adopted the convention of dividing the Earth side of the Moon into quadrants. The north pole of the Moon is at the top, and the south pole is at the bottom. The views in this volume show the Moon in this way. The lunar **prime meridian** is an imaginary line that runs north to south and marks 0° **longitude**. Other meridian, or longitude, lines run 180° east (+) and west (−) of the prime meridian. The equator marks 0° and runs east to west. Lunar **latitudes** measure to 90° north (+) and 90° south (−) of the equator. Note that the western edge of the Moon is on the left. This is based on the rotation of the Moon, so that a person on the Moon would see the Sun rise in the east and set in the west.

THE MOON'S VARIED TERRAIN

Craters

The second-most-visible lunar features are craters. It has been estimated that more than 30,000 craters can be observed on the Earth side of the Moon with a small telescope. There are actually millions of craters on the Moon. The size of lunar craters ranges from a few inches to several hundred miles across. Craters as small as approximately 1.8 miles (3km) across can be observed using a small telescope. The smallest craters visible through large Earth-based telescopes are about the size of football stadiums. Lunar

> ▼
>
> This view of the cratered surface of the Moon was taken from Apollo 10. The large dark areas near the center are the Sea of Tranquility, the Sea of Serenity, and the Sea of Storms. Notice all the craters in the vicinity of the terminator, the line of demarcation between night and day, dark and light, on the Moon's surface.

orbiters and landers have shown craters much smaller. The best time to observe craters is when the Moon is not full, and the best place to look for them is along the shadowed edge known as the **terminator**, where the lit and unlit parts of the Moon appear to meet on the lunar surface. The steep angle of the sunlight at this point highlights every-

This is an artist's rendering of the cratering of the Moon's surface billions of years ago. The heat generated by large impacts on the lunar surface may have melted the Moon's crust, forming the lunar seas.

thing along this line; even the smallest craters cast long shadows.

Some of the largest craters are called **walled plains** because of their large smooth surfaces. Most of the craters, however, are smaller **impact craters**, formed by meteorites or asteroids colliding with the Moon. Evidence also points to volcanic origins for some craters.

Craters are usually named after famous scientists and personalities. One of the most famous craters is Copernicus, named after the sixteenth-century Polish astronomer Nicolaus Copernicus (1473–1543) **(Vol. 5, pp. 14–15)**. Described as a **ringed mountain**, the crater Copernicus features long lines in a sunburst pattern called **lunar rays**. Lunar rays are

◀ The crater Copernicus with its many lunar rays. Copernicus appears to make the nose of the Man in the Moon. This crater is 57.7 miles (93km) in diameter and is believed to have been formed by a giant impact one billion years ago.

▲ The crater Tycho is found near the southern (bottom) edge of the Moon. It appears to have lunar rays extending more than 1,000 miles (1,609km) in all directions. During the Full Moon this crater can be seen with a pair of high-powered binoculars or with a small telescope.

straight lines that radiate out from the center of some craters. They are trails of ejected debris that appear bright against the backdrop of the lunar surface. In Copernicus's case some of the lunar rays extend almost 500 miles (800km) from it in all directions. Copernicus is located near the center of the Earth side of the Moon and marks the end of the "nose" of the Man in the Moon. This crater's walls rise over 17,000 feet (582m) above the lunar plain. Its diameter is 57.7 miles (93km), and it is more than 2.33 miles (3.76km) deep. On the inside of the crater numerous landslides are visible, and in the center are several mountains. Copernicus is one of the youngest craters, having formed only one billion years ago.

Another famous and easily identifiable crater is Tycho, named after the sixteenth-century Danish astronomer Tycho Brahe (1546–1601) **(Vol. 5, p. 15)**. It appears as a circular depression 53 miles (85km) wide and 3 miles (4.85km) deep. There is a central mountain 1 mile (1.6km) high. This is also one of the younger craters, estimated to be only 100 million years old. Tycho is located in the southern hemisphere near the prime meridian and is best observed near the time of the Full Moon when the crater is highly illuminated. It also has lunar rays, which extend almost a thousand miles (1,600km) in all directions. The rays can easily be seen using binoculars or a small telescope. They cross over lunar features, which means they are younger than the parts of the Moon they cross.

One of the largest craters on the Earth side of the Moon is named Clavius, called after Father Clavius, a Jesuit astronomer who was

THE MOON'S VARIED TERRAIN

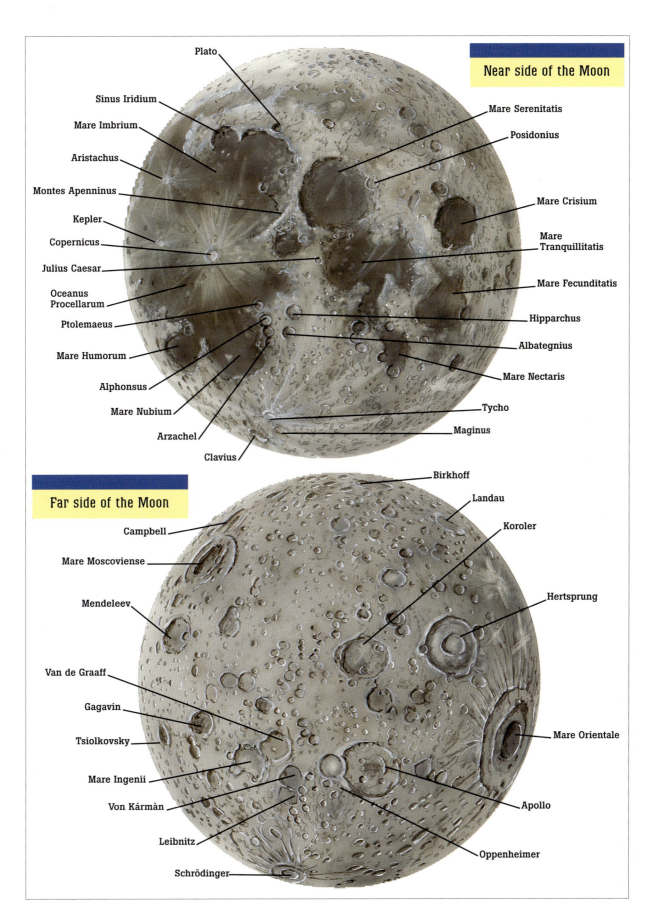

THE MOON'S VARIED TERRAIN

▲ This view of the southern (bottom) edge of the Moon shows thousands of craters. The large crater Clavius, 125 miles (200km) in diameter, features a small semicircle of craters across its floor.

▲ This is a close-up of a large lunar crater taken by the Apollo 11 astronauts. Many craters have not been named; this one is known by the designation IAU (for International Astronomical Union) #308 and is 50 miles (80km) in diameter.

a contemporary of Galileo. It appears on the southern hemisphere, near the southern limb. It is 140 miles (225km) in diameter, and it has several smaller craters forming a crescent on its floor. Clavius is sometimes referred to as a walled-plain crater **(p. 35)**.

Craters often appear to line up, forming a chain. In the central part of the lunar disk there is a large crater named Ptolemaeus (after the second-century Alexandrian astronomer Claudius Ptolemaeus), with a diameter of 95 miles (153km), that has two smaller craters lined up with it called Alphonsus and Arzachel (for two other early astronomers). These easily identified craters are almost exactly in the center of the Moon's Earth side.

One of the newest discoveries involving Moon craters was announced in 1994 after scientists found traces of water-based ice in polar craters. The discovery was made by a military spacecraft named Clementine that was placed into orbit around the Moon. The shape of the orbit allowed the satellite to pass directly over the lunar polar regions. Using a radio transmitter on board the spacecraft, scientist were able to bounce radio waves deep into some of the polar craters that never receive sunlight. As the waves bounced back to Clementine, they indicated the presence of frozen water. In the cold of space the temperature in these craters never climbs above freezing. It is possible that a comet hit the moon millions of years ago and deposited ice on the lunar surface. Any ice deposited on the Moon would melt in the heat of the Sun, unless the ice was deep inside one of these polar craters.

THE MOON'S VARIED TERRAIN

Mountains

Lunar mountains are among the brightest areas visible on the Moon. The southern highland of the Moon appears as a collection of valleys, peaks, ridges, and craters. It appears as a wavy and rough place, without any smooth surfaces at all, except for the floors of some of the larger craters. Some of the southern mountains rise to over 26,000 feet (7,925m). Relative to the size of the Moon itself, these are giant mountains. There are also mountain ranges separating many of the lunar seas and other features.

The most obvious lunar range of mountains is the Apennines, known as Montes Apenninus, on the southeastern border of Mare Imbrium. There are more than three thousand peaks in this impressive range of mountains, which is 160 miles (257km) wide and runs 600 miles (966km) along the lunar surface. The tallest of the Apennines is Mount Huygens, which is more than 20,000 feet (6,095m) tall. These mountains, some of the largest on the Moon, can best be viewed during lunar quarter-phases, when they cast long shadows **(p. 40)**. This range forms the "bridge of the nose" of the Man in the Moon. In the northwestern part of the range Apollo 15 landed near a sinuous rill known as Rima Hadley.

Above the Apennines, and appearing almost as an extension of them, are the Montes Caucasus (Caucasus Mountains). They are separated from the Apennines by a 31-mile (50km) lava flow. The Caucasus Mountains also form the northeastern wall of Mare Imbrium and separate Mare Serenitatis from Imbrium. The tallest peak in the northern end of the Caucasus is located near the crater Eudoxus and is 19,000 feet (5,791m) tall. The Alps are found near the walled plain Plato, which is located north of Mare Imbrium and the Apennines. These mountains contain several hundred peaks, and several of these peaks are more than 10,000 feet (3,048m) tall. The most famous feature in the lunar Alps is the great Alpine Valley, which cuts though the range in a northeasterly direction from the crater Plato.

◀ The lunar mountain range known as the Apennines is visible across the bottom of this photograph. Also shown are Eratosthenes, the crater at the end of the range, and the craters Archimedes, Autolycus, and Aristillus, visible in the upper right. The smooth area in the upper left is the Sea of Rain (Mare Imbrium), which holds the crater Timocharis.

THE MOON'S VARIED TERRAIN

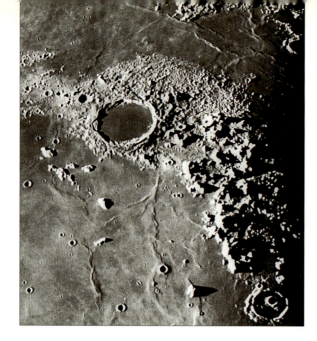

▲ The deep shadows along the terminator reveal many craters and mountains. Notice how the shadows appear long and pointed. This gave many early astronomers the impression that the Moon's mountains were very tall and pointed, but now we know that is an illusion created by the steep angle of the sunlight hitting the Moon's surface; lunar mountains are more like smooth hills. The large crater with the smooth floor is Plato. The mountain with the long shadow is Mons Piton.

Just north of the crater Copernicus are the Montes Carpatus (Carpathian Mountains). This range runs 180 miles (290km), and has peaks 7,000 feet (2,134m) high. On the eastern edge of Mare Serenitatis and the northern edge of Mare Tranquillitatis is the large mountainous area known as Montes Taurus (Taurus Mountains). These mountains, some of which are 10,000 feet (3,048m) tall, appear as an irregular region of block mountains. Other mountain ranges include Montes Haemus (Haemus Mountains), near Mare Serenitatis; Montes Harbinger (Harbinger Mountains), between Oceanus Procellarum and Mare Imbrium; and Montes Teneriffe, near the crater Plato. The Moon contains numerous other mountain ranges that are identified on lunar maps.

There are also isolated mountain peaks on the lunar surface. In Mare Imbrium, near Plato, there is an 8,000-foot (2,400m) mountain named Mons Pico. It is easily observed with a small telescope, casting a long shadow during the First or Last Quarter Moon.

Mons Piton, another notable mountain peak that is visible with a small telescope, is found in Mare Imbrium just west of the crater Cassini. It rises 7,000 feet (2,250m) above the sea floor and casts a long shadow when seen in the terminator **(pp. 34–35)**. Several large craters also have high mountain peaks in their centers. The craters Copernicus, Tycho, Gassendi, and Theophilus all have peaks that cast long shadows in sunlight.

LUNAR SHADOWS

Shadows of mountains and craters often appear long, dark, and pointed. They give the impression that lunar features are tall, slender, sharp spikes, but this is not the case. The lunar mountains are shaped like smooth sand dunes or rolling hills. It is the strong angle of the sunlight that causes the long shadows. Think about your own shadow in the late afternoon; as the Sun is setting, your shadow makes you look like you are 30 feet (9m) tall and very thin.

THE MOON'S VARIED TERRAIN

MAPPING THE MOON

The earliest known "modern" lunar map was drawn by English astronomer William Gilbert (1544–1603) around 1600. His map was very simple and included the light and dark areas of the Moon that are visible to the naked eye. Gilbert thought the dark areas were land and the light areas were seas. Gilbert's map was not published until some years after his death in 1603. Later the invention of the telescope made Moon mapping more accurate. Galileo **(Vol. 3, p. 10)** was one of the most famous early lunar map makers. In 1610 he used one of the first telescopes to conduct lunar studies. He noted that the Moon was covered with "spots" and was not perfectly smooth. He saw valleys and mountains, and was able to compute the heights of some of the lunar mountains by measuring their shadows. Galileo made several lunar drawings, but none of them was published; they are known from later examinations of his personal notes.

In 1647 Johann Hevelius (1611–1687), a Polish amateur astronomer, mapped the lunar surface with some degree of accuracy. He was able to measure the lunar mountains and record details that Galileo could not observe. His moon map clearly showed the details of craters, lunar rays, and mountains ranges. He also gave many of the lunar features names, some of which are still used on modern moon maps.

In 1651 Italian astronomer Giovanni Riccioli (1598–1671) published a lunar map with a new system of naming lunar features. He gave many of the seas their names, including Mare Imbrium and Mare Tranquillitatis **(p. 32)**, and established the tradition of naming craters after famous personalities. His names are still

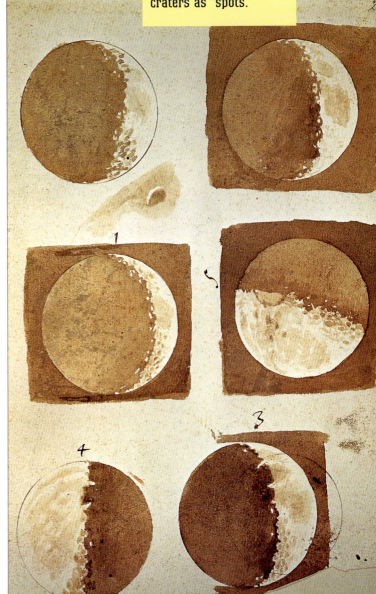

▼ These drawings of the Moon were made by Galileo around 1610. Notice how he drew the lunar craters along the terminator. Using a small telescope, Galileo saw that the surface was not smooth and noted that there were mountains; he referred to the craters as "spots."

▲ Riam Ariadaeus, a lunar rill, is visible in this photograph; it appears as a straight feature near the Sea of Tranquillity. The large crater on the left is Julius Caesar.

▲ This is a view of the crater Schmidt taken from Apollo 10. This crater is 7 miles (11km) in diameter. The shadowy area is the eastern edge of the crater.

used today, and the Moon's features bear more than two hundred of Riccioli's selected names. Many of the most famous scientists and astronomers have lunar craters named after them. Galileo's name was given to a small crater on the western edge of Oceanus Procellarum, and Tycho Brahe's name was given to the most prominent visible crater. Riccioli named a crater for himself and one for his assistant Grimaldi; these craters are prominently positioned on the western edge of the Moon. Important lunar surface studies and charts were produced by the French astronomer Giovanni Cassisi (1714–1784) and German astronomers Tobias Mayer (1723–1762) and Johann Schröter (1745–1816), to name a few. They have all been honored by having their names attached to lunar craters.

The first photographic maps of the Moon were made in 1840. These **daguerreotypes** (an early kind of photograph made on a copper plate) of the Moon were small in size and showed few details, but marked the way for future photographic atlases. Within ten years of the first daguerreotype pictures other photographs were taken recording the different phases of the Moon. There was a limit to the quality of these photographic maps because Earth's atmosphere always interfered, causing blurring. A space mission to map the Moon was the only way to obtain detailed maps. In 1959 Luna 3, a Soviet space probe, took the first successful lunar photographs, including some taken on the dark side. In 1964 the first U.S. space probe, Ranger 7, returned more than four thousand photographs before crashing in Mare Nubium. A series of five lunar orbiters followed, and the entire lunar surface was photographed in detail.

THE APOLLO EXPEDITIONS

Many people have dreamed of exploring the Moon in person, from ancient worshipers to early science fiction authors and movie makers. That dream started to become reality in 1961, when President John F. Kennedy made a famous speech:

"I believe this nation should commit itself to achieving the goal, before this decade is out, of landing a man on the Moon and returning him safely to Earth. No single space project in this period will be more impressive to mankind, or more important for the long-range exploration of space; and none will be so difficult or expensive to accomplish."

This announcement established a national goal and set the time scale for the mission: in fewer than ten years humankind would reach the Moon. The challenge involved more than just going to the Moon—it required the creation of a new space program unlike anything ever seen before. Kennedy's announcement sparked the United States into developing new materials and technology.

In the late 1950s most of the space missions focused on the deployment of Earth-orbiting satellites, though the Soviets also had plans to send probes to the Moon. The "space race" between the Unites States and the Soviet Union was on. The United States attempted to be the first nation to send a human into space with project Mercury, but the Soviets got there first. On April 12, 1961, Yuri Gagarin became the first person ever to orbit Earth. **(Vol. 8, pp. 23–25)** On May 5, 1961, twenty-three days after Gagarin, the U.S. placed Alan Shepard into suborbital flight. Three weeks later President Kennedy announced the Moon mission, and the space race took off with increased vigor.

The single-man space capsule of project Mercury was to be followed directly by the Apollo program, but several new technologies were not yet in place. The Gemini program was launched to develop the necessary technologies. In order to reach the Moon, astronauts had to learn to work in space over long periods of time and learn how to maneuver vehicles in space. Accordingly, astronauts in project Gemini practiced **space-docking (Vol. 8, pp. 34–36)** with target vehicles and perfected other skills needed to accomplish project Apollo's goals of landing on the Moon. The Gemini program ended in 1966 and was followed by project Apollo. Meanwhile, unmanned space probes were busy exploring the Moon, and **lunar orbiters** began mapping the Moon's surface in search of potential landing sites

At the same time the Mercury, Gemini, and Apollo teams were being prepared, new space hardware in the form of larger rockets and lunar landing craft was being developed. A trip to the Moon would require a very large rocket capable of delivering two spacecraft into Earth orbit and enough fuel to further propel the spacecraft to the Moon **(Vol. 8, pp. 37–45)**. Project Mercury had used a

◀ Apollo 7 lifts off from Cape Kennedy Space Center, Launch Complex 34. Astronauts Donn Eisele, Walter Cunningham, and Walter Schirra performed an Earth orbit test flight of the Apollo equipment in October 1968.

small Redstone rocket that stood 83 feet (25.2m) tall and later switched to a slightly larger Atlas rocket borrowed from the United States Air Force's Intercontinental Ballistic Missile (ICBM) program. The Atlas stood more than 95 feet (28.9m) tall. Project Gemini used a slightly larger Titan II rocket that could carry a larger payload. The Titan II stood more than 118 feet (36m) tall.

To work, project Apollo would need a rocket much larger and more complex than any ever built before. The Saturn rocket was developed to meet this need. The Saturn IB was a two-stage rocket used to carry unmanned and manned Apollo spacecraft into Earth orbit in preliminary flights before the Moon voyage. The rocket stood over 141 feet (43m) tall and weighed 1,300,000 pounds (590,000kg). The initial launch was February 26, 1966, and was the first of four launches that year. The Saturn V, with the Apollo spacecraft, stood more than 363 feet (111m) tall and delivered 7,750,000 pounds (34,500,000 newtons) of thrust at liftoff. It was the most powerful rocket the United States had ever built and the largest rocket in the world.

The Saturn V rocket also required assembly and launch facilities capable of handling the heavy equipment. The Cape Canaveral Space Center in Florida was selected as the site for the Moon mission. This center would later be named the Kennedy Space Center.

On January 27, 1967, a tragic fire killed three Apollo astronauts as they were training inside their Apollo capsule. The Apollo program was temporarily stopped as systems were redesigned and tested. Almost two years later, on October 11, 1968, Apollo 7 was launched, carrying three astronauts into Earth orbit. And on December 21, 1968, Apollo 8 carried three

SATURN V ROCKET

The Saturn V rocket consists of several **stages**, or sections. Each stage has fuel tanks and one or more rocket engines. As the fuel is exhausted in each stage it is jettisoned. This makes the rocket less massive as it travels along and enables the remaining stages to travel faster with less fuel.

1. First Stage: Five F-1 power plants, producing a total thrust of 7,500,000 pounds (34,500,000 newtons), furnish the main thrust. The engines and their fuel (a mix of liquid oxygen and liquid hydrogen) make up most of the first stage. An interstage located on top of the first stage contains the first-stage electronics and fuel to accelerate the second stage slightly forward, so that fuel will flow in the absence of gravity. This is important because in zero gravity the fuel would just float and not flow properly into the rocket engine.

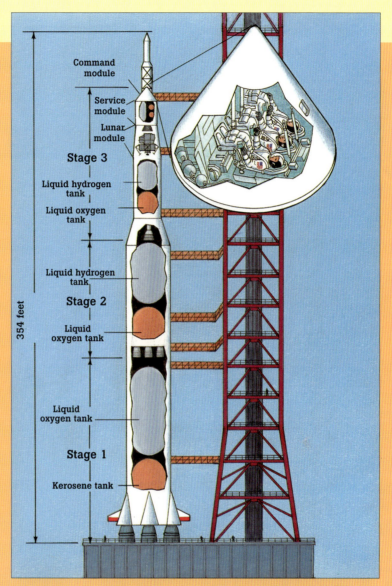

2. Second Stage: Five J-2 engines, producing more than 1,000,000 pounds (4,500,000 newtons) of thrust. Liquid hydrogen and liquid oxygen are the propellants.

3. Third Stage: One J-2 engine, its controls, and fuel. Instrument unit and a **tunicated** (multisectional) conical structure to house and protect the lunar module during flight.

4. Lunar module: Two-stage landing craft to carry two astronauts to the surface of the Moon and return them to lunar orbit.

5. Service Module: Holds fuel cells for electrical power, tanks, and support systems. A single, restartable rocket engine is used for propulsion and maneuvering in space after the third stage is jettisoned.

6. Command Module: Includes the escape tower that may be used at time of launch in case of emergency, the capsule where crew quarters and rocket controls are located, and the service module that contains the fuel and rocket engine used to return the astronauts from the Moon to Earth orbit. Note: the only part of the rocket that returns to Earth is this capsule.

THE APOLLO EXPEDITIONS

◀ Astronaut Neil Armstrong prepares for the flight of Apollo 11. He became the first human to walk on the Moon, July 20, 1969.

men into orbit around the Moon. Frank Borman, James Lovell, and William Anders became the first humans to take a trip to the Moon. They did not land, but their flight proved that a trip to the Moon was possible **(Vol. 8, pp. 38–39)**.

Apollo 9 was the first complete Apollo spacecraft, which is to say it featured the command, service, and lunar modules **(Vol. 8, p. 38)**. Launched on March 3, 1969, Apollo 9 and its astronauts journeyed only as far as Earth orbit. They practiced maneuvering the lunar lander in space and docking and undocking with the command ship. They also tested all the portable life-support systems to be used by the astronauts on the lunar surface.

Apollo 10 was the full dress-rehearsal for the lunar landing. Astronauts traveled to the Moon, docked with the lunar lander, and flew the lander within 9.7 feet (3m) of the lunar surface. No landing was made, but the landing site for the Apollo 11 mission was photographed and studied. The first

◀ The Apollo 10 command module with astronaut John Young orbits the far side of the Moon some 60 miles (97km) above the lunar surface. This photograph shows the lunar module with astronauts Stafford and Cernan aboard as they survey the surface for a landing site from a distance of 50,000 feet (15,240m).

◀ Astronaut Charles Conrad, Jr., unpacks equipment on the Moon. Apollo 12 landed several feet from Surveyor III, a spacecraft that had landed on the Moon two and a half years earlier. Notice the smooth surface of the landing site in the Sea of Storms.

landing on the Moon occurred on July 20, 1969, when Neil A. Armstrong and Edwin E. "Buzz" Aldrin piloted the lunar lander Eagle into the Oceanus Tranquillitatis. Millions of people listened on Earth as Armstrong described the landing:

"Down 2½. Forward. Forward. Good. 40 feet, down 2½. Picking up some dust. 30 feet, 2½ down. Faint shadow. 4 forward, drifting to the right a little, 6 down a half, forward. Drifting right. Contact light. Okay, engine stop, ACA out of detent. Modes control both auto, descent engine command override off. Engine arm off. 431 is in."

There was a pause and then the words, "Houston, Tranquility Base here. The Eagle has landed."

Astronaut Neil Armstrong was the first human being to touch the Moon. He stepped onto the lunar surface at exactly 10:56 P.M.

EDT His words as he stepped on the lunar surface were, "That's one small step for man, one giant leap for mankind." An estimated five hundred million people watched as a dream came true—a human had finally visited another place in space, the Moon. Armstrong may have taken the first step, but more than 300,000 people in the space program had helped him take that step, making it a collaborative accomplishment.

Astronaut Michael Collins remained in Columbia, the command service module, in lunar orbit, while Aldrin accompanied Armstrong. Armstrong remained on the Moon for 2 hours, 31 minutes, and 37 seconds, and Aldrin roughly 40 minutes fewer. The Apollo 11 command module safely returned to Earth on July 24, 1969, carrying all three astronauts and 47.8 pounds (21.7kg) of Moon rocks and dust.

THE APOLLO EXPEDITIONS

◀ After their near-fatal mission, the astronauts of Apollo 13—from left to right, Fred Haise, John Swigert, and James Lovell—achieved splashdown in the Pacific Ocean, where they were rescued by the U.S. Navy on April 17, 1970.

Apollo 12 landed in Oceanus Procellarum **(pp. 31–32)** on November 19, 1969. Richard F. Gordon Jr. was the command module pilot and stayed in lunar orbit. Charles Conrad Jr. and Alan L. Bean spent 31½ hours on the lunar surface. They practiced a precision landing near the Surveyor III spacecraft, which had landed on the Moon more than 2½ years earlier, and the crew retrieved several pieces of the Surveyor III craft. Then, with the rescued materials and 75.8 pounds (34.4kg) of lunar matter, the lunar module Intrepid rejoined the Apollo 12. The crew and cargo safely arrived on Earth on November 24.

Apollo 13 was launched on April 11, 1970. Two and one-half days later an onboard explosion caused a loss of all oxygen stored in the service module. The oxygen was necessary for the fuel cells to produce electric power as well as for the maintenance of life support. The crew was forced to abort the mission. They evacuated the command module, Odyssey, and used the lunar lander, Aquarius, attached to the command module as a lifeboat. Through ingenuity and resourcefulness the crew and the ground technicians returned the crippled vehicle to Earth. This was the closest the United States had ever come to losing a crew during a space mission **(Vol. 8, pp. 42–43)**.

Apollo 14 was launched on January 31, 1971. Its mission was to land in the Fara Mauro highlands of the Moon, which had been the planned landing site for Apollo 13. Alan Shepard, the United States's first man in space, was the command pilot. Astronauts Shepard and Edgar D. Mitchell spent 33 hours on the Moon and conducted two **extravehicular activities (EVAs) (Vol. 8, p. 30; Vol. 9,**

THE APOLLO EXPEDITIONS

p. 49). Apollo 14 returned to Earth on February 9 with 94.5 pounds (42.9kg) of lunar rocks. The command module was named Kitty Hawk, after the historic site in North Carolina where, in 1903, the Wright brothers had become the first humans to achieve powered flight. The lunar lander was named Antares, after the brightest star in the constellation Scorpius, which the astronauts could see out their window as they landed.

Apollo 15 was commanded by astronaut David R. Scott, and the command module pilot was Alfred M. Worden. Launched on July 26, 1971, this mission carried the first "car" to the Moon. The **lunar roving vehicle (LRV)** enabled astronauts David Scott and James B. Irwin to maximize their time on the Moon. They spent 66 hours and 55 minutes on the lunar surface and conducted three EVAs.

Apollo 15 returned on August 7 with 173 pounds (76.8kg) of Moon rocks, more than double the amount returned by Apollo 11. The command ship for Apollo 15 was named Endeavour, after the sailing vessel used by the eighteenth-century English navigator and explorer Captain James Cook. The lunar lander was named Falcon, for the official U.S. Air Force mascot. The crew were all Air Force pilots.

Apollo 16 made the fifth landing on the Moon and was commanded by astronaut John W. Young. Launched on April 16, 1972, it landed in the southern highlands near the crater Descartes. Astronauts Young and Charles Duke stayed on the Moon for more than twenty hours and performed three EVAs, collecting more than 213 pounds (94.7kg) of Moon rocks. Apollo 16's lunar module was named after the constellation Orion. The command module was

This photograph of the Apollo 14 lunar module, Antares, was taken by the astronauts during their second EVA of the mission. Tracks left by the **modularized equipment transporter (MET)** can be seen leading away from the lunar module.

APOLLO FLIGHTS

Flight	Dates	Crew	Mission	Landing Site
Apollo 1-6	May 13, 1964– April 4, 1968	Unmanned test flights*	N/A	
Apollo 7	October 11, 1968	Donn F. Eisele, Walter Cunningham, Walter M. Schirra	Earth orbit EVA	
Apollo 8	December 21-27, 1968	James A. Lovell Jr., William A. Anders, Frank Borma	Lunar orbit	
Apollo 9	March 3-13, 1969	James A. McDivitt, David R. Scott, Russell L. Schweickart	Earth orbit and test of lunar module	
Apollo 10	May 18-26, 1969	Thomas P. Stafford, John W. Young, Eugene A. Cernan	Lunar orbit and test of lunar module	
Apollo 11	July 16-24, 1969	Neil A. Armstrong, Michael Collins, Edwin E. Aldrin Jr.	First lunar landing	Oceanus Tranquillitatis
Apollo 12	November 14-24, 1969	Charles Conrad Jr., Richard F. Gordon, Alan L. Bean	Landing	Oceanus Procellarum
Apollo 13	April 11-17, 1970	James A. Lovell Jr., John L. Swigert, Fred W. Haise Jr.	Mission aborted due to onboard explosion; astronauts returned safely	
Apollo 14	January 31– February 9, 1971	Allen B. Shepard, Stuart A. Rossa, Edgar D. Mitchell	Landing	Fara Mauro highlands
Apollo 15	July 26– August 7, 1971	David R. Scott, Alfred M. Worden, James B. Irwin	Landing	Apennine Mountains
Apollo 16	April 16-27, 1972	John Young, Thomas K. Mattingly, Charles M. Duke Jr.	Landing	Descartes highlands
Apollo 17	December 7-19, 1972	Eugene A. Cernan, Harrison H. Schmitt, Ronald E. Evans	Landing	Tairis-Littrow

*Astronauts Virgil I. Grissom, Edward H. White II, and Roger B. Chaffee were killed in a fire that erupted inside a command module during ground testing on January 27, 1967. They were scheduled to fly the first manned Apollo mission.

THE APOLLO EXPEDITIONS

named Casper, after the cartoon ghost, by the crew.

The final landing on the Moon was made by Apollo 17. Launched on December 7, 1972, the lunar lander module Challenger touched down in a valley south of the crater Littrow, near the eastern edge of Mare Serenitatis **(p. 32)**. While command module pilot Ronald E. Evans orbited in the command service module America, astronauts Eugene A. Cernan and Harrison H. Schmitt spent more time on the Moon than any other Apollo astronauts had. They performed longer EVAs (22 hours' worth) and collected more Moon rocks, 243 pounds (110.5kg), than any other mission. At the end of the last EVA astronaut Cernan left a plaque on the Moon. The plaque reads, "Here man completed his first exploration of the Moon December 1972 A.D. May the sprit of peace in which we came be reflected in the lives of all mankind."

Cernan stepped off the Moon's surface at approximately 12:40 A.M. EST, December 14, 1972. He was the last person to touch the surface of the Moon. After Apollo the U.S. space program turned its attention to developing a reusable space craft—the space shuttle **(Vol. 9)**.

▶ The Sun can be seen shining brilliantly above the lunar module Antares. Notice the gold foil wrapping of the spacecraft, included to protect it from the Sun's rays.

APOLLO LANDING DATES AND COORDINATES

Mission	Landing Date	Latitude	Longitude
Apollo 11	July 20, 1969	0 deg 67 min N	23 deg 49 min E
Apollo 12	November 19, 1969	3 deg 12 min S	23 deg 23 min W.
Apollo 13	April 17, 1970	Returned to Earth	
Apollo 14	January 31, 1971	3 deg 40 min S	17 deg 28 min E
Apollo 15	July 30, 1971	26 deg 6 min N	3 deg 39 min E
Apollo 16	April 21, 1972	9 deg 0 min N	15 deg 31 min E
Apollo 17	December 11, 1972	20 deg 10 min N	30 deg 46 min E

CONCLUSION

Now that human beings have finally visited the Moon and have sophisticated equipment for collecting information about our satellite, some of our questions about the Moon have been answered. But just the same, this lunar exploration has raised new questions. There is still a debate about how the Moon was formed, for example **(pp. 9–16)**. And astronomers are still puzzled about the events that formed the lunar seas and mountains **(pp. 28–40)**. Overall, we have visited only a tiny fraction of the Moon's surface; there are thousands of lunar sites waiting to be explored.

As you look at the Moon on a clear night, it might still be difficult to believe human beings have actually realized the age-old dream of traveling there. Now there is a new dream: to build a space colony on the Moon from which exploration might continue. With the establishment of a permanent base on the Moon humans might take the next step and fulfill another dream: to go to other planets and someday even visit other stars.

GLOSSARY

Apollo The program name given to the U.S. manned space program, 1968 to 1972. The main objective was to enable a man to visit the Moon and return to Earth.

Ascending Node See **node**

Barycenter The center of mass around which two celestial bodies orbit.

Bedrock The solid surface of rock underlying unconsolidated surface material such as soil or dust.

Blue Moon When a month has two full moons, the second full Moon is referred as a Blue Moon.

Capture Model Theory stating the Moon was caught in orbit by the gravity of Earth.

Center of Mass The point in a body or system of bodies around which the whole mass may be considered concentrated.

Centrifugal Force The force that tends to push an object outward from a center of rotation.

Collision Capture Model Theory of the Moon's formation through captured by the Earth's gravity after it collided with several smaller moons.

Conservation of Energy The principle that the total energy of an isolated system remains constant.

Core The central, innermost area of an object.

Crater A circular depression usually found on cosmic bodies with solid surfaces. May result from volcanic activity or impacts from asteroids. They are most notably found on planetary moons.

Crescent Moon Visible before and after the **New Moon–Waxing Crescent** in the evening, and **Waning Crescent** in the morning.

Dark side of the Moon Term often incorrectly associated with the "back" of the Moon; a term describing the side of a celestial body that is opposite the Sun.

Density The mass of a substance per unit of volume.

Descending Node See **node**

Dome (lunar) Raised portion of the lunar surface that may be the result of volcanic action.

Double Planet Model Theory that the Moon formed at the same time as (and near) the Earth.

Double Planet System Theory that some planets and moons can be said to represent two planets orbiting around a common **barycenter**.

Eclipse The total or partial obscuring of one celestial body by another, which occurs when one body passes into the shadow of the other.

Ecliptic The apparent line on which the Sun moves among the stars. It is also known as the plane of the solar system. The Moon and planets appear to follow close to the ecliptic.

Ellipse A somewhat flattened circle traced by a moving point whose distance from two fixed points (foci) remains constant.

Equatorial Plane The imaginary plane extending from the center off the Earth through the equator into space. It divides the celestial sphere into north and south.

Equilibrium A state of balance.

Extravehicular Activity (EVA) Activity of astronauts outside a vehicle or space craft.

Fault A fracture in the continuity of a rock formation or surface feature.

First Quarter Moon Rising before sunset, the Moon is 90° from the Sun and appears to be only half-illuminated. At this phase only one-quarter of the Moon's surface is visible from Earth.

Fission Model

Full Moon Occurs when the Moon is 180° from the Sun. It rises at sunset, is visible all night, and sets at sunrise.

Giant Impact Model Theory the Moon may have been flung into orbit around Earth by a Mars-sized object that crashed into the Earth.

Gibbous Moon Occurs when the Moon is between **Quarter** and **Full**. Moon is **Waxing Gibbous** as it moves toward Full and is **Waning** Gibbous after Full.

Gravitational Force The mutual attraction between two masses directed along the line of their centers.

Impact Crater Crater formed by the striking of one body against another.

Last Quarter Moon Occurs when the Moon is three-quarters of the way through its orbit of Earth, approaching its original starting position between Earth and the Sun. During this phase it appears to be half-illuminated (on the opposite half from the **First Quarter Moon**). It rises at midnight.

Latitude Angular distance north or south of the equator or the ecliptic (when in reference to a celestial body).

Libration The apparent rocking motion of the Moon as it orbits around the Earth. The effect enables Earthbound observers to see more than 50% of the lunar surface at different times in the Moon's orbit.

Limb Astronomically, a term for the outer visible edge of a celestial disk, as in the limb of the Moon.

Longitude Angular distance measured east and west of a prime meridian. Earth's prime meridian passes through Greenwich, England.

Lunar Calendar An early kind of calendar based on lunar phases; such calendars did not keep pace with Earth's seasons and so were abandoned, replaced by seasonal calendars.

Lunar Month The time taken by the Moon to complete one orbit of Earth from one New Moon to the next: 29 days, 12 hours, 44 minutes, 2.9 seconds.

Lunar Orbiter A series of five lunar landers, all of which were successfully placed in lunar orbit and mapped almost the entire lunar surface during 1966 and 1967.

Lunar Roving Vehicle (LRV) A small electric car taken to the Moon for the first time on Apollo 15.

Lunation See **lunar month**

Mantle Layer of Earth between the crust and core.

Maria Latin name for "sea," used to describe features on the Moon, specifically dark areas made of iron and rich basalt rock.

Nebula A diffused mass of interstellar dust or gas or both.

New Moon Occurs when the Moon is directly between the Sun and Earth. A solar **eclipse** may occur if the Sun is located at one of the lunar **nodes**.

Nodes The points at which the Moon's orbit intersects the **ecliptic**, to which it is inclined 5°. The point at which the Moon crosses the ecliptic moving north is the **ascending node**, and the same point moving south is the **descending node**.

Occultation When one celestial body causes another celestial body to disappear from view.

Penumbra A partial shadow.

Penumbral eclipse A lunar eclipse that occurs when the Moon enters the partial shadow of the Earth.

Phase The amount of the illuminated disk of a body (the Moon) that shines by reflected sunlight and is visible from Earth.

Primary The central celestial body (a planet or star) relative to other celestial bodies in orbit around it. The body with the largest mass is generally termed the primary.

Prime meridian The zero degree of longitude from which other longitudes are measured to the east and west.

Refract To deflect from a straight line, usually used to describe a path of light.

Regolith The crushed and fragmented rock layer that covers the surface of the Moon and other planetary bodies that lack an atmosphere. The layer is a result of millions of years of meteorite impacts. The lunar regolith is approximately 32 to 275 feet (10 to 100m) deep.

Rays (lunar) Bright elongated streaks radiating from certain craters on the Moon that may be made of material ejected from impacts.

Rills A canyon or gorge found in the surface of moons or planets.

Ringed Mountain Term often applied to a large crater structure that contains a central mountain or group of mountains.

Roche limit The distance limit between a moon and planet after which a moon will be destroyed by gravitational stress; considered to be 2.4 times the radius of the planet.

Rotational Energy The energy possessed by a body due to its spin.

Saros The period of 18 years, 11 days that it takes for the **nodes** of the Moon's orbit to complete one revolution around the ecliptic. It was used by ancient astronomers to predict eclipses.

Sidereal Month The time taken by the Moon to complete one revolution around Earth with respect to the background stars: 27 days, 7 hours, 43 minutes, 11.6 seconds.

Sidereal Period The time required for a planet or satellite to complete one revolution around its **primary**, with respect to the background stars.

Solar Calendar Calendar based on the movement of the Earth and the apparent movement of the Sun. Measures what is known as a tropical year: 365 days, 5 hours, 48 minutes, and 45.51 seconds.

Summit Pits Craterlike openings in the tops of some lunar mountains.

Synchronous Rotation The turning of a celestial body such that the same side is always facing the body around which it revolves.

Synodic Month See **lunar month**

Synodic Period The time required for a planet or satellite to complete one revolution around its **primary** as observed from the primary. In the case of the moving Earth, this period will be longer than the sidereal period.

Terminator The boundary between the day and night sides of a moon or planet. Along the terminator the angle of sunlight is strongest, and it is the best place for observing details of the Moon.

Tidal Friction The resistance of motion between two celestial bodies undergoing gravitational influence. In a closed system one celestial body will accelerate as the other slows down.

Totality Phase of an eclipse when one celestial body is covered by the shadow or disk of another.

Umbra The darkest part of the conical shadow of a celestial body. Also the darkest part of a sunspot.

Unstable Equilibrium

Walled Plains Large crater with high walls and a flat floor.

Wane To decrease in size or extent; the period from Full Moon to New Moon.

Wavelength Distance between successive crest troughs of a wave.

Wax To increase in size or extent; the period from New Moon to Full Moon.

Wrinkles (lunar) Areas of the lunar surface that are folded or creased, having the appearance of wrinkles.

GLOSSARY

SET INDEX

Volume numbers appear in **bold**. Page references in *italics* refer to pages with photographs and illustrations.

A

Aldrin, Edwin "Buzz," **2**: 47; **8**: 36, 40, 41; **9**: 6, 26; **10**: 6, *7*
Aliens, **6**: 47
Allen, Joseph, **9**: *40*
Alpha Centauri, **6**: 17, 18; **7**: 50
Anders, William, **2**: 46; **8**: 38; **10**: *8*
Apollo spacecraft, **2**: 9, 28, *31*, 43–51; **8**: *6*, 32, *33*, *40;* **9**: 6, 8; **10**: 7, *30*, 31, *32*
Armstrong, Neil, **2**: *46*, 47; **8**: 36, 40, 41; **9**: 6, 26; **10**: *6–7*
Asteroids, **1**: 7, 46–49; **2**: 11, 31; **3**: 46; **4**: 13, 31, 52; **7**: 11, 21; **8**: 51, 52; **12**: 49–52
Astronauts, **2**: *14*, 43, 46, 47, 48, 50; **8**: 26, 27, *28*, 30, *33*, *35*, 38; **9**: 6, 26, *28*, 36, *40–41*, *44–46*, *48*, *50*, *52*; **11**: *7*, *20–22*, 26, *30*, 31, *37*, *39*, 42
    commanders, **10**: 15–16
    early, **10**: 9–11
    mission specialists, **10**: 15, 17
    moon landings, **10**: 6
    payload specialists, **9**: 51; **10**: 15, 18
    pilots, **10**: 15, 16
    selection process, **10**: 12–15
    training, **10**: 6, 7, 19–21
Astronomers, **6**: 7; **7**: 8–10, 13–15, 17–21
    amateur, **7**: 21
    in education, **7**: 20
    radio, **7**: 18
    research, **7**: 18
    theoretical, **7**: 20
Astronomical units (AU), **1**: 27, 40; **3**: 33; **6**: 17; **8**: 15
Astronomy, **11**: 6
    ancient, **7**: 8–10
    early, **5**: 12–14
    modern, **5**: 14–15
    radio, **7**: 34–36
    satellites, **7**: 45–49
Astrophysics, **7**: 17, 21

Atlantis shuttle, **9**: *7*, *23*, 26, *32*, *43*, 49; **10**: 24; **11**: *38*, 39
Atlas spacecraft, **10**: 11
Auroras, **1**: 32, *33;* **4**: 24

B

Bean, Alan L., **2**: 48; **11**: *23*
Belayev, Pavel I., **8**: 30
"Big Bang," **6**: 41, 48; **7**: 48, 49
Black holes, **6**: 13, *27*, 28–29, 31, 46, *47*, 49; **7**: 20; **12**: 43
Borman, Frank, **2**: 46; **8**: 38; **10**: *8*
Brahe, Tycho, **1**: *13*, 14; **2**: 36, 42; **5**: 15
Brilliant Pebbles program, **12**: 47
Bursch, Daniel, **10**: *46*

C

Cabana, Robert, **9**: *41*
Caisson's disease, **10**: 35
Calendars, **2**: 18; **5**: 12; **7**: 9
Cameron, Kenneth, **10**: *8*, 16
Cape Canaveral Space Center (Florida), **2**: 44; **8**: *14;* **9**: *16*, 17
Carpenter, Scott, **8**: *29;* **10**: *12*
Carr, Gerald, **11**: 24
Cassini probe, **4**: *14*, 15, 39; **8**: 52, *53;* **12**: 13, 47
Challenger shuttle, **9**: *13*, 26, *29*, 34, 35, *42*, 47
Chilton, Kevin, **9**: *32;* **11**: *31*
Clementine probe, **12**: 47, 48
Clifford, Michael, **9**: 41; **10**: *7;* **11**: 31
Collins, Michael, **2**: 47; **8**: 36, 40, 41; **9**: 26; **10**: 6, 7
Columbia shuttle, **9**: *6–7*, *14–16*, 22, 24, 26, *32*, *37;* **10**: 16, *47;* **12**: *42*
Comets, **1**: 7, 37–42; **2**: 11; **4**: 35, *52*, 53; **5**: 26; **6**: 30; **7**: 21, 40; **8**: 51, 52; **12**: 49–52
    Giacobini-Zinner, **12**: 51
    Grigg-Skjellerup, **12**: 51
    Hale-Bopp, **1**: *38*, 40, *41;* **7**: 52–53
    Halley's, **1**: *37*, 39–40; **3**: 31; **7**: *46;* **8**: 51; **12**: 51
    Hyakutake, **2**: *50;* **12**: 50
    Ikey-Seki, **1**: *42*
    IRAS-Araki-Alcock, **7**: 46
    Kohoutek, **11**: 24
    open orbit, **1**: 37
    parts, **1**: 38–39

    periodic, **1**: 37, 38
    Shoemaker-Levy, **1**: *38;* **4**: *23*–24; **7**: 37, 40, 42
    West, **1**: *37*
Conrad, Charles Jr., **2**: *14*, *47*, 48; **10**: 41; **11**: *7*, *20*, 22
Constellations, **5**: 6, 9–10; **6**: 11, 15; **7**: 6
    Aquarius, **7**: *44*
    Aquila, **5**: 42–43
    Auriga, **5**: 28
    Big Dipper, **5**: 32–33
    Boötes, **5**: 37–38
    Canis Major, **5**: *29*, 30
    Canis Minor, **5**: *30*
    Cassiopeia, **5**: 47–48
    Centaurus, **11**: 33
    Cepheus, **5**: 48–49
    Cetus, **5**: 52
    Cygnus, **1**: 11; **5**: 40–41; **7**: *47;* **11**: 33–34
    Draco, **5**: 35
    Gemini, **5**: *31*, 32
    Hercules, **5**: 45–46
    Leo, **5**: 35–37
    Little Dipper, **5**: 33–34
    Lyra, **5**: 39–40
    Ophiuchus, **5**: 44
    Orion, **1**: *11;* **5**: *23*, 24–25; **6**: 15; **7**: 42
    Pegasus, **1**: 11; **5**: 50–51
    Perseus, **5**: 52–53
    Pisces, **5**: 51–52
    Sagittarius, **5**: 43–44; **6**: 40; **7**: 34
    Scorpius, **5**: 43
    Serpens, **5**: 44–45
    Sirius, **7**: 50
    Taurus, **5**: *27*, 28; **6**: 26
    Triangulum, **6**: 39, *43*
    Ursa Major, **1**: 11; **5**: *32*, 33
    Ursa Minor, **5**: 33–34
    Vela, **11**: 33
    Virgo, **1**: 11; **5**: 38–39
Cooper, Gordon, **10**: *12*
Cooper, Leroy Jr., **8**: *29*
Copernicus, Nicolas, **2**: 36; **5**: *14*, 15; **7**: 13, 14
Copernicus spacecraft, **12**: 43
Cosmonauts, **2**: 43; **8**: 23, 30, 33; **11**: *7*, 9, *15*, 26, *27*, *30*, 31, *32–33*, *35*, 36, *37*, *39*, 42
    early, **10**: 9–11
    selection process, **10**: 13–15
    training, **10**: 21–22
Crippen, Robert, **9**: *32*

D

Deep Space Network, **12**: 13
Discovery shuttle, **9**: 24, *25,* 26, *27,* 46, 47; **10**: *8, 14–15,* 18, *30,* 31, *50;* **11**: 39; **12**: 41
Doppler effect, **6**: 29

E

Earth, **1**: 14; **3**: 32–38; **7**: 50
  atmosphere, **1**: 18–19; **3**: 33–34
  composition, **3**: *32*
  diameter, **3**: 32
  gravitational force, **2**: 12; **3**: 19
  mass, **2**: 14
  observing, **3**: 12–13
  orbit, **2**: 19; **3**: 32
  ozone layer, **12**: 25
  rotation, **2**: 11, 18; **8**: 14
  seasons on, **3**: 34–36
  terrain, **1**: *19;* **3**: 6, 19, 36–38
  volcanoes on, **3**: 20, 37
Eating, **9**: 23; **10**: 42–44; **11**: 6, 22, 31, 43
Echo satellite, **12**: *32*
Eclipses, **7**: 22
  annular, **1**: 34
  Baily's beads, **1**: 35
  diamond ring effect, **1**: *35*
  lunar, **2**: 24–27
  partial, **1**: 33; **5**: 15
  solar, **1**: 7, 29, 33–36
  total, **1**: 7, 33, 34, 36
Einstein, Albert, **1**: *28;* **7**: *20;* **12**: 21
Endeavour shuttle, **9**: *16, 18,* 26, 28, 51; **10**: *46;* **11**: 39; **12**: *36*
Energy, **7**: 8
  electromagnetic, **1**: 29
  measuring, **4**: 11
  movement of, **7**: 16
  nuclear, **11**: 46
  photons in, **7**: 48
  providing, **11**: 47
  solar, **1**: 32, 33; **11**: 50
Enterprise shuttle, **9**: 26
Equinoxes, **3**: 35, 36
European Space Agency, **1**: 26; **8**: 51; **10**: 43; **12**: 22, 39, 43, 44
Explorer satellites, **8**: 21, 22, 23
Extravehicular activities, **2**: 48, 49, 51; **8**: 31, 34; **9**: 28; **10**: 15, 36, *40;* **11**: 19, 21, 23

Extravehicular Mobility Unit, **10**: 20–21, *36–38,* 39, *40, 41*
Extreme Ultraviolet Explorer (EUVE), **12**: 43, *44*

F

Faint Object Camera, **1**: 26; **12**: 42
Fast Auroral Snapshot satellite, **12**: 49
Fedorov, Viktor, **11**: *37*
Feoktistov, Konstantin, **10**: *13*
Foale, C. Michael, **10**: 36
Fullerton, C. Gordon, **9**: *23*

G

Gagarin, Yuri, **2**: 43; **8**: 23, *24;* **10**: *9, 13;* **11**: 14
Galaxies, **1**: 49; **5**: 7; **6**: 6, 7, 36–39; **7**: *38, 42;* **12**: *41*
  active, **6**: 44, 45
  Andromeda, **5**: 8, 51; **6**: 30, 39, *42,* 44; **7**: 51
  birth of, **6**: 40–42
  Centaurus A, **6**: 44
  Cygnus A, **6**: 45
  distances to, **8**: 15
  elliptical, **6**: 36–37, 41, 44, *46*
  irregular, **6**: 37, *38*
  Local Group, **6**: 42–43, 44
  M100, **7**: 24
  Magellanic, **6**: *37–38,* 44; **7**: 51; **11**: 34
  Milky Way, **5**: 18; **6**: *7,* 8, *17,* 18, 39–40; **7**: *15,* 25, 34, *51*
  NGC 2363, **7**: *37*
  number of, **7**: 44
  Omega Centauri, **7**: *19*
  radio, **6**: 45
  Sombrero, **5**: *39*
  spiral, **1**: *51;* **5**: 51; **6**: 36, 40, 41, 42
Galilei, Galileo, **1**: 24; **2**: 30, 42; **3**: *10;* **4**: 8, 25, 35, 45; **5**: 17–19; **7**: 13–14, 28
Galileo probe, **2**: 16; **3**: *12,* 13, 31; **4**: 14–15, 20, 27, 31; **8**: 52; **9**: *43,* 47; **12**: 8, *12,* 20, 47, 50
Garriott, Owen, **11**: *21–23*
Gemini spacecraft, **2**: 43; **8**: 29, *31, 34–36;* **10**: 35
Geostationary Operational Environmental Satellites, **12**: 30–31
Gibson, Edward, **11**: 24, 25

Giotto probe, **1**: 39; **8**: 51; **12**: 51
Glenn, John, **8**: 28, *29;* **10**: 11, *12*
Global Positioning System (GPS), **12**: 27, 33
Globalstar satellite, **12**: 35, 37
Goddard, Robert, **8**: *18*
Goddard High Resolution Spectrograph, **9**: 47
Godwin, Linda, **11**: *31*
Gravity, **1**: 8; **6**: 28; **8**: 7, 9–13. *See also* Microgravity
  artificial, **9**: 53; **11**: 10, 11, 49
  assist, **3**: 12; **8**: 12, 13, 52; **12**: *45,* 46
  explanation of, **7**: 20
  false, **10**: 29
  g-forces, **10**: 31–33
  solar, **1**: 6
  in space, **12**: 11
  tidal friction, **3**: 47
Greenhouse effect, **1**: 17; **3**: 27, 33, 34
Grissom, Virgil "Gus," **8**: 26, 27, *29;* **10**: *12*

H

Habitat Wheel, **11**: *10*
Haise, Fred, **2**: *48;* **8**: 43
Harris, Bernard Jr., **9**: *46;* **10**: *36, 50*
Hawking, Stephen, **7**: 20
Heat shields, **8**: 12, 28–30
Heliopause, **8**: 51; **12**: 53
Helms, Susan, **9**: *39*
Herschel, William, **4**: 40, 42; **7**: *14,* 15
Hoffman, Jeffrey, **9**: *48, 50–51*
Hubble, Edwin, **7**: 24–25
Hubble Space Telescope, **1**: 8, 26; **4**: 7, 11, 35, 41, 47; **6**: 41; **7**: 18, *24,* 47; **8**: 48; **12**: *39–40,* 41, 49
  accomplishments with, **7**: 39–44
  repairs to, **9**: 44–47
  size, **7**: 38
Huygens, Christian, **1**: 24; **4**: 35
Hygiene, **10**: 44–45; **11**: 18, 30

I

Infrared Astronomy Satellite (IRAS), **7**: 45–46; **12**: *43*
Infrared Space Observatory (ISO), **12**: 43
International Geophysical Year, **8**: 19; **12**: 7, 25

International Maritime Satellite Organization, **12**: 37
International Space Station, **11**: 25, 40–43
International Ultraviolet Explorer, **7**: 46–47
Iridium satellite, **12**: *35,* 37
Irwin, James B., **2**: 49; **8**: *44*
Ivins, Marsha, **9**: *23, 52*

J

Jansky, Karl, **7**: *34*
Jemison, Mae, **9**: 51–52
Johnson Space Center (Houston), **10**: 19–20, 39
Jupiter, **1**: 14; **4**: *6,* 16–31; **7**: 12, 14–15, *37,* 39, 50
   atmosphere, **4**: 18–20
   cloud bands, **4**: *9,* 10, 20
   comet collision with, **7**: 40, 42
   composition, **4**: 16–18
   gravity on, **4**: 16; **12**: 45
   Great Red Spot, **1**: *22;* **4**: *12,* 20–21
   missions to, **1**: 22; **4**: 11–14 *15;* **8**: 51–52; **9**: 43, 47; **12**: 8, 12, 45–46, 50, 52
   moons, **3**: 12; **4**: 8, *12,* 25–28, 29, *30–31;* **7**: 40; **8**: 52; **12**: 50
   observing, **4**: 8–10
   period, **4**: 8
   probes of, **8**: 12
   ring system, **1**: 23; **4**: *22–23*
   rotation, **4**: 8, 16
   size, **4**: 6
   storms on, **1**: 22; **4**: 21
   terrain, **1**: *22;* **3**: 19

K

Kennedy Space Center (Florida), **2**: 44; **9**: 7, *16, 22;* **11**: 20, 23
Kepler, Johannes, **1**: 13; **5**: *16,* 17; **8**: 7
Kerwin, Joseph, **10**: 41; **11**: *7, 20,* 22
Kuiper Belt, **1**: 40–41; **4**: 53

L

Laika (space dog), **8**: 20–21
Leonov, Aleksei A., **8**: 30–31; **10**: *10*
Liberty Bell spacecraft, **8**: 26
Light
   infrared, **12**: 38–39

rays and waves, **7**: 45
spectrum, **7**: 16
speed of, **1**: 28; **4**: 11; **6**: 16; **7**: 50–51
ultraviolet, **3**: 14; **11**: 33
visible, **5**: 19; **6**: 6; **7**: 8, 16; **12**: 38–39, 42
wavelengths, **2**: 26; **12**: 38
years, **5**: 24; **6**: 11, 17, 18; **8**: 15
Linenger, Jerry, **9**: 23, 41; **11**: 37
Lousma, Jack, **11**: 23
Lovell, James Jr., **2**: 46, 48; **8**: 38, 43; **10**: 8
Lowell, Percival, **1**: 20; **3**: 48; **4**: 49
Lucid, Shannon, **10**: 25; **11**: 30–31, 39
Lunar Excursion Module (LEM), **8**: 38–41, 42, *44*
Lunar Orbiter, **8**: 32
Lunar roving vehicle, **2**: 49

M

Magellan probe, **1**: 18; **3**: *15,* 25, 28, 31; **9**: 47; **12**: *12*
Mariner spacecraft, **1**: 16, 20; **3**: 14, 16, 24, 44, 46; **8**: 48, *49,* 50; **12**: 17
Mars, **1**: 14; **3**: 39–51; **7**: 12, 50
   atmosphere, **1**: 19; **3**: 11, 16, 17, 40–41, 48–49
   color, **3**: 11, 18
   diameter, **3**: 39
   distance to, **3**: 39–40
   gravity on, **3**: 19, 40
   ice caps, **1**: *20;* **3**: *45*
   life on, **3**: 48–49
   missions to, **3**: 7; **8**: 53; **12**: *48*
   moons, **3**: 46, *47*
   observing, **3**: 11, 16–18
   period, **3**: *42*
   rotation, **3**: 11, 40
   seasons on, **3**: 42
   storms on, **3**: 41
   temperature, **3**: 16, 40
   terrain, **1**: 19–20; **3**: 6, *16,* 17, *18,* 19, *39,* 43–44
   volcanoes on, **3**: 20, 43–44
Mars Global Surveyor, **1**: 20; **3**: 17, 18, 46; **8**: 53; **12**: *48,* 49
   Sojourner rover, **3**: *17,* 50–51
Mars Observer, **3**: *16;* **12**: 49
Mars Pathfinder, **1**: 20; **3**: *17,* 18, 46, *50,* 51; **8**: 53; **12**: 8, 49

McArthur, William, **10**: *49*
McAuliffe, Sharon Christa, **9**: *30*
Mercury, **1**: 14; **3**: 21–24; **7**: 50
   atmosphere, **1**: 16; **3**: 14, 22–23
   distance to, **3**: 21
   gravity on, **3**: 19
   magnetic field, **3**: 24
   missions to, **3**: 14; **8**: 50
   observing, **3**: 14
   orbit, **3**: *22*
   rotation, **3**: 21–22
   temperature, **3**: 23
   terrain, **1**: *16—17;* **3**: 6, 14, 19, *21—24*
   volcanoes on, **3**: 20
Mercury spacecraft, **2**: 43–44; **8**: 26–28, 29, 30, *31,* 34; **10**: 11
Messier, Charles, **5**: 25–26
Meteorites, **1**: 44; **2**: 11, 31; **3**: 50, *51;* **7**: 16, 50
Meteors, **1**: 42–45; **5**: 46–47, 53; **7**: 6
Microgravity, **9**: 39, 40; **10**: 18, 20, 25, 50; **11**: 8, 25, 31
   body positioning in, **10**: 30
   effect on humans, **10**: 27–29, 32–33
   gray out, **10**: 33
   space sickness in, **10**: 30
   working in, **10**: 29–30
Milky Way, **5**: 18, *30;* **6**: 7, 8, *17,* 18, 30, 39–40; **7**: *15,* 25, 34, *51*
Mir Space Station, **8**: 33; **10**: *13–14,* 16, *21, 24,* 25, *27,* 50; **11**: 9, *26, 30, 31, 38–39;* **12**: 36
Mission Control, **9**: 32; **10**: 23
Mitchell, Edgar D., **2**: 48
Moon, **2**: 6–52; **3**: 38
   capture model, **2**: *12*
   collision capture model, **2**: *12,* 13
   craters, **2**: *34–38*
   double planet model, **2**: 13–15
   early probes, **8**: 32
   eclipses of, **2**: 24–25, *26,* 27
   fission model, **2**: 9–11
   formation of, **2**: 9–16, 31
   giant impact model, **2**: *15*
   maps, **2**: 33, 41–42
   mass, **2**: 14
   missions to, **2**: 14, 43–51; **8**: 37–44
   mountains, **2**: *39–40*
   orbit, **2**: 17–18, 24
   period, **2**: 11
   phases, **1**: 12; **2**: *18–21*
   seas, **2**: *30–32*

SET INDEX

synchronous rotation, **2:** 22, *23,* 24
terrain, **2:** *7–8, 11,* 13, *28–29;* **5:** *18,* 19
tidal friction, **2:** 17
Multi-Object Spectrometer, **9:** 47
Musgrave, F. Storey, **9:** *44–45*

N

NASA. *See* National Aeronautics and Space Administration
National Aeronautics and Space Administration, **3:** 50; **8:** 52; **9:** 15; **10:** 7, 9, 15, 16, 17; **11:** 11, 18, 42, 48; **12:** 36, 39, 44, 47, 51, 52
Near-Earth Rendezvous spacecraft, **12:** 51, 52
Near-Infrared Camera, **9:** 47; **12:** 41–42
Nebulae, **1:** *8,* 10–11; **2:** 9; **5:** 6, 7; **6:** *17,* 19, 23, 30, 40; **7:** 25, 42
  absorption, **5:** 25
  Bridal Veil, **6:** *35*
  Cat's Eye, **7:** *39*
  dark, **5:** 25; **6:** 33, 35
  diffuse, **6:** 33
  emission, **6:** 32–33
  Horsehead, **5:** *25*
  Lagoon, **5:** *44*
  North American, **1:** *11*
  Orion, **1:** *11, 53;* **5:** 8, *25;* **7:** *39*
  Pelican, **6:** *34*
  planetary, **6:** 25, *32;* **7:** *39*
  reflection, **6:** 33
Nelson, George, **10:** *17*
Neptune, **1:** 14; **4:** 6, 45–48; **7:** 12, 39, 40, 50–51
  atmosphere, **4:** 46–47
  color, **1:** *25*
  composition, **4:** 46–47
  Great Dark Spot, **4:** *46,* 47
  missions to, **4:** 13, 14; **8:** 51–52; **12:** 8, 52
  moons, **4:** 8, 47–48
  observing, **4:** 10–11
  orbit, **1:** 25
  period, **4:** 8
  ring system, **4:** 47
  rotation, **4:** 8
  storms on, **7:** 40
  temperature, **1:** 25
  terrain, **3:** 19
Newman, James, **10:** *51*

Newton, Isaac, **5:** *19;* **7:** 20, 30; **12:** 9, 15
North Star, **3:** 35, 36; **7:** 22

O

Observatories, **3:** *48*
  ancient, **7:** *9,* 22
  Egyptian, **7:** 9, 22
  Keck (Hawaii), **7:** *33*
  Lick, **7:** 30
  Mauna Kea (Hawaii), **7:** *25, 36,* 45
  Mayan, **7:** 9, 22
  McDonald Observatory (Texas), **7:** 22
  modern, **7:** 22
  permanent, **7:** 22
  side-by-side, **7:** 33
  Stonehenge (England), **5:** *11;* **7:** 22
  United States Naval Observatory (Washington), **7:** 25
  Yerkes (Wisconsin), **7:** 25
Ochoa, Ellen, **10:** *17*
Onufrienko, Yuri, **11:** *27, 32, 35, 39*
Oort Cloud, **1:** 40; **4:** 53; **6:** 30
Orbits, **12:** 7
  asteroid, **1:** 48
  elliptical, **2:** 19; **8:** 7; **12:** 15
  geosynchronous, **9:** 42; **12:** 31–33
  Moon/Earth, **2:** 17–18
  outer planets, **4:** *9*
  planetary, **1:** 12–15
  satellites, **12:** 22–23
  solar, **12:** 46
  speeds, **1:** 13–14
  tilts, **1:** 12–13
  velocity in, **8:** 14

P

Pioneer spacecraft, **1:** *7;* **3:** 14, 31; **4:** 11, 13, *19,* 37; **8:** 32, 48, *51;* **12:** *9,* 46, 53
Planetariums, **7:** 20
Planets, **1:** 9
  atmosphere, **8:** 11
  densities, **4:** 7
  diameters, **4:** 8
  distances to, **3:** 18
  formation of, **7:** 42–43
  inferior, **3:** 11
  inner, **3:** 6–52; **4:** 6
  Jovian, **4:** 6, 7
  moons, **4:** 8

motion of, **7:** 12,13
orbits, **1:** 12–15; **3:** 10; **8:** 7
outer, **1:** 21–26; **4:** 6–55; **7:** *12,* 39
periods, **4:** 7–8
proplyds, **7:** 42
retrograde motion, **5:** 14; **7:** 12–13
rotation, **4:** 7–8
superior, **3:** 11
temperatures, **4:** 7
terrestrial, **1:** 16–20; **3:** 19; **4:** 6
volcanic activity on, **3:** 20; **7:** 40
Plate tectonics, **3:** 19, 30, 37; **4:** 29
Pluto, **1:** 14; **4:** 6–7, 49–51; **7:** 12, 42, 50
  composition, **4:** 50
  missions to, **4:** 13
  moons, **4:** 8, *49,* 50–51; **7:** 42
  observing, **4:** 10–11
  period, **4:** 8
  rotation, **1:** 26; **4:** 8
Pluto Express, **4:** 15; **7:** 42
Pogue, William, **11:** *24*
Polyakov, Valery, **10:** 14; **11:** 26
Popovich, Pavel, **10:** 13
Progress spacecraft, **11:** 16, 28, 31, 33
Proton rockets, **11:** 15
Protoplanetary disks, **7:** 42
Protostars, **7:** 42
Ptolemy, Claudius, **2:** 38; **5:** 14; **7:** 12–13
Pulsars, **5:** 28; **6:** 26–27; **12:** 43, 53

Q

Quasars, **6:** 13, *44–45, 46, 47*

R

Radiation, **6:** 7; **7:** 16. *See also* Rays and waves
  atmospheric, **8:** 21
  background, **7:** 48–49
  cosmic, **11:** 10, 45
  electromagnetic, **6:** 27; **7:** 50; **12:** 42
  high-energy, **7:** 47–48
  infrared, **6:** 13; **12:** 41–42
  ultraviolet, **6:** 13; **12:** 43
Ranger spacecraft, **2:** 42; **8:** 32
Rays and waves. *See also* Light
  gamma, **7:** 8, 45, 47; **12:** 42
  infrared, **7:** 16, 38, 45; **11:** 33
  light, **7:** 17, 45
  microwave, **7:** 16–17, 45, 48–49

radio, **5:** 28; **6:** 44, 46; **7:** 8, 16–19, 45; **12:** 42
ultraviolet, **1:** 18; **7:** 16, 17, 38, 45
x-rays, **7:** 16, 45, 47; **11:** 33; **12:** 39, 42–44
Relativity, **1:** 28; **7:** 20; **12:** 21
Ride, Sally, **9:** *40*
Rockets, **8:** 9–18; **9:** 10; **12:** 9, 11
  antimatter, **11:** 46
  booster, **8:** 13–14, 16–17, 34, 37–38, 46; **9:** 17, *19,* 28
  conventional, **8:** *15*
  fuel, **8:** 18
  gunpowder, **8:** 16–17
  hybrid, **8:** 18
  Jupiter, **8:** 21
  liquid propellant, **8:** 18
  military, **8:** 19
  multistage, **2:** 44, *45;* **8:** 12; **11:** 11; **12:** *14, 16*
  orbits, **8:** 9
  Proton, **11:** 15; **12:** *11*
  Redstone, **2:** 44
  retrorockets, **8:** 30, 31
  Saturn, **2:** 44, *45;* **8:** 37–38, 40, 42, 44; **11:** 18, 20
  thrust in, **8:** 16
  Titan, **2:** 44; **8:** *17*
  Titan-Centaur, **8:** *50*
  trajectories, **8:** 9
  X-15, **9:** *12*

S

Salyut Space Station, **11:** 12–17
Satellites, **5:** 8; **7:** 8; **12:** 6–54
  astronomical, **7:** 45–49; **12:** 37–46
  BeppoSAX, **12:** 44
  building, **12:** 17–18
  Clementine, **12:** 47–48
  communications, **12:** 13, *24,* 26, 31–32, 35
  composition, **12:** 8–13
  Compton Gamma Ray Observatory, **12:** 44
  dead, **12:** 36
  deployment, **12:** 17
  early, **8:** 19–23
  Early Bird, **12:** 32
  Earth Remote Sensing, **12:** 22
  Echo, **12:** *32*
  Explorer, **8:** 21–23
  Extreme Ultraviolet Explorer (EUVE), **12:** 43, *44*
  Fast Auroral Snapshot, **12:** 49
  Geostationary Operational Environmental Satellites, **12:** 30–31
  geosynchronous, **12:** 23–24
  Ginga, **12:** 43
  Global Positioning System, **12:** 27, *33, 34*
  Globalstar, **12:** 35, 37
  Infrared Astronomy Satellite (IRAS), **12:** 43
  Infrared Space Observatory (ISO), **12:** 43
  Iridium, **12:** *35,* 37
  launching, **9:** 42–44
  Meteor, **12:** *25*
  military, **12:** 26–27, 30, 34
  polar-orbiting, **12:** 22
  powering, **12:** 10
  power station, **11:** 47
  propelling, **12:** 14
  Roentgen Satellite, **12:** 43
  Solar, Anomalous, and Magnetospheric Particle Explorer, **12:** 49
  Solar and Heliospheric Observatory (SOHO), **12:** 46, 50
  Spartan, **12:** *38*
  speed of, **12:** 15
  Sputnik, **8:** *19–21,* 22–23; **9:** 10; **10:** 11; **12:** *8*
  Syncom, **12:** 24
  systems, **12:** 22–24
  Telstar, **12:** 32
  testing, **12:** 21
  uses, **12:** 25–37
  Vanguard, **8:** 22–23
  weather, **12:** 23, 26, 30, *31*
  X-Ray Multi-Mirror Mission (XMM), **12:** 43
  X-Ray Timing Explorer (XTE), **12:** 43
Saturn, **1:** 14; **4:** *6,* 32–39; **7:** 12, 39, 50
  atmosphere, **1:** 23; **4:** 34–35
  color, **1:** 23
  composition, **4:** 32, 34
  missions to, **4:** 11–13; **8:** 51–52; **12:** 8, 13, 46, 52
  moons, **4:** 8, *14, 33,* 37, *38–39;* **8:** 52, *53*
  observing, **4:** 8–10
  period, **4:** 8
  ring system, **1:** *21, 23,* 24; **4:** *9,* 10, *33–37*
  rotation, **4:** 8
  size, **4:** 6
  terrain, **3:** 19
Saturn rockets, **2:** 44, *45;* **8:** 37–38, 40, 42, 44; **11:** 18, 20
Schirra, Walter Jr., **8:** *29;* **10:** *12*
Searfoss, Richard, **9:** *32;* **11:** *31*
Shepard, Alan Jr., **2:** 43, 48; **8:** 26, *29;* **10:** 9, *10,* 12
Shuttle Imaging Radar, **12:** 30
Single Stage to Orbit system, **8:** 47, 48
Skylab Space Station, **1:** 29; **8:** *44;* **10:** 41, 49; **11:** 7, *10,* 18, *19,* 20, *21–24,* 25
Slayton, Donald, **8:** *29;* **10:** *12*
Sleeping, **10:** *47;* **11:** 6, 18, 30
Solar, *See also* Sun
  eclipses, **1:** 7, 29, 33–36
  energy, **1:** 32–33; **11:** 50
  flares, **1:** *32;* **6:** *10;* **11:** *25*
  granules, **1:** 32
  gravity, **1:** 6
  panels, **11:** 22, *47*
  prominences, **1:** *27, 36*
  sails, **11:** 46
  telescopes, **11:** *21,* 25
  wind, **1:** 32
Solar, Anomalous, and Magnetospheric Particle Explorer, **12:** 49
Solar and Heliospheric Observatory (SOHO), **12:** 46, 50
Solar system, **1:** 6; **7:** 14–15
  birth of, **1:** 8–11
  limits of, **4:** 14
  probes outside of, **12:** 52–53
Solar Thermal Vacuum Chamber, **12:** 21
Solovyev, Anatoli, **10:** *13*
Solstices, **3:** 35, 36; **5:** 11; **7:** 22; 9
Soyuz spacecraft, **11:** 14, 28
Space
  animals in, **10:** 11
  colonies, **11:** 11, 48, 50–51
  deep, **12:** 11, 13
  eating in, **8:** 33; **9:** 23; **10:** 42–44; **11:** 6, 22, 31, 43
  effects on humans, **8:** 33; **9:** 39–41; **10:** 25–29, 42–47; **11:** 8–10, 49
  emergencies, **2:** 44, 48; **8:** 36, 37, 42; **9:** 34; **10:** 24, 41; **11:** 15, 20, 35–37
  exercising in, **8:** 33; **10:** 45; **11:** 30

experiments in, **10:** 49–51
gravity in, **12:** 11
hygiene in, **10:** 44–45; **11:** 18, 30
junk, **12:** 36
living in, **10:** 42–48
long-term stays in, **11:** 8–10
race, **2:** 43; **9:** 6; **10:** 9
recreation in, **11:** 32
settlements, **11:** 48–50
sickness, **9:** 38; **10:** 30
simulations, **10:** 19–21
sleeping in, **10:** 47; **11:** 6, 18, 30
stresses in, **10:** 22–26; **11:** 8
suits, **10:** 33–39; **11:** 18, 20
talk, **12:** 11
toilets in, **9:** 21, 23; **10:** 44; **11:** 18
walks, **8:** 35; **9:** 47, 49; **11:** 22
working in, **10:** 49–51
Spacecraft
   Apollo, **2:** 9, 28, *31,* 43–51; **8:** *6, 32, 33, 37,* 38, *39–40, 42;* **9:** 6, 8; **10:** 7, 30, 31, 32
   Atlas, **10:** 11
   Copernicus, **12:** 43
   Cosmos, **11:** 16
   Delta Clipper, **8:** 47
   distance in, **8:** 15
   docking, **2:** 43, 46; **8:** 34–35, 44; **11:** 16, 28, 45
   exercising in, **10:** *46*
   Freedom, **8:** 26
   Gemini, **2:** 43; **8:** 29, *31,* 34–36; **10:** *35*
   and gravity, **10:** 27
   hypersonic, **11:** 50
   Liberty Bell, **8:** 26
   Luna, **8:** 32
   Lunar Orbiter, **8:** 32
   Mariner, **1:** 16, 20; **3:** 14, 16, 24, 31, 44, 46; **8:** 48–50; **12:** 17
   Mercury, **2:** 43–44; **8:** 26–31, 34; **10:** 11
   Near-Earth Rendezvous, **12:** 51
   payload on, **8:** 13; **9:** 18; **12:** 14
   Phobos, **3:** 46
   Pioneer, **1:** *7;* **3:** 14, 31; **4:** 11, 13, *19,* 37; **8:** 32, 48, *51;* **12:** *9,* 46, 53
   Progress, **11:** 16, 28, 31, 33
   Ranger, **2:** 42; **8:** 32
   reentry burn, **8:** 12
   Single Stage to Orbit, **8:** 48
   sleeping in, **10:** *47*
   Soyuz, **8:** *33;* **11:** 14, 28

   Surveyor, **8:** 32
   toilets in, **10:** 45
   travel, **8:** 6–53
   Ulysses, **9:** 49; **12:** 44, *45, 46*
   Vega, **3:** 31
   Venera, **3:** 27, 31
   Viking, **1:** 20; **3:** 16, 18, 46–47, 49; **7:** 39; **8:** 49–50
   Voskhod, **8:** *31*
   Vostok, **8:** 23, *24–25,* 29–30, *31;* **10:** 11
   Voyager, **4:** 13–14, 18, 20, 22, 30, 37, 42, 47–48; **6:** 18; **7:** 40; **8:** 12, *13,* 51; **12:** 8, 46, *53*
   walks, **8:** *35*
   Zond, **8:** 32
Spacelab, **9:** *13, 18;* **10:** 18
Space Shuttle(s), **7:** 41; **8:** *10,* 14, *45;* **9:** 6–52; **10:** 7; **11:** 28; **12:** *12,* 17
   Atlantis, **9:** *7,* 23, 26, *32,* 43, 49; **10:** 24; **11:** *38,* 39
   Challenger, **9:** *13,* 26, *29,* 34, *35, 42,* 47; **10:** 33
   Columbia, **9:** *6–7, 14–16, 19,* 22, 24, 26, *32, 36–37;* **10:** 16, *47;* **12:** *42*
   components, **9:** 17–29
   Discovery, **7:** 37; **9:** 24, *25,* 26, *27,* 46–47; **10:** *8, 14–15,* 18, *30,* 31, *50;* **11:** 39; **12:** 41
   Endeavour, **9:** *16, 18,* 26, 28, *38,* 44, 51; **10:** *46;* **11:** 39; **12:** 36
   Enterprise, **9:** 26
   launching, **9:** 30–38
   living on, **9:** 50–53
   naming, **9:** 26
   reusable, **8:** 45–46; **9:** 10–11, 28; **10:** 15
   Single Stage to Orbit, **8:** 47
   Voyager, **7:** 51
Space Stations, **10:** 15; **11:** 6–54; **12:** 11
   civilian, **11:** 14–15
   first-generation, **11:** 14–15
   International Space Station, **10:** *42;* **11:** 40–43
   joint efforts, **11:** 16, 37–39
   military, **11:** 14–15
   Mir, **8:** 33; **10:** 13, *14,* 16, *27,* 50; **11:** *6–7,* 9, *26,* 28–31, *34–35, 38–39;* **12:** 36
   repair work on, **11:** 20–23, 35–37
   Salyut, **11:** 12–17

   second-generation, **11:** 16–17
   Skylab, **1:** 29; **11:** *18–24*
Space Telescope Imaging Spectrograph, **9:** 47; **12:** 42
Space Transportation System, **9:** 8
Spectrographs, **7:** 38
Spectrometer, infrared, **11:** 33
Spectroscopes, **4:** 38; **7:** 16, 28
Spectrum, **5:** 19; **7:** 16, 45
   electromagnetic, **7:** 8, 16–19, 38
Sputnik satellites, **8:** *19–21,* 22–23; **9:** 10; **10:** 11; **12:** *8*
Stars
   Betelgeuse, **7:** 50
   binary, **5:** 38; **6:** *21;* **7:** 14–15
   birth of, **6:** *14,* 19–22
   black dwarf, **1:** 31
   blue giant, **5:** 24
   brightness, **5:** 14, 21; **6:** 11–13
   Cepheid variables, **7:** 44
   circumpolar, **5:** 32–33
   clusters, **1:** *8;* **4:** 52; **5:** 8; **6:** *9,* 21–22, 40
   color, **6:** 13, 16
   constellations, **7:** 6
   death of, **6:** 23–26
   distances to, **6:** 15; **8:** 15
   double, **1:** 50–51
   formation of, **7:** 21; **12:** 43
   islands, **6:** 36–39
   late, **12:** 43
   multiple, **5:** 7; **6:** 21–22
   naming, **5:** 24
   nemesis, **1:** 50–51
   neutron, **11:** 34
   observing, **6:** 13
   protostars, **7:** 42
   red dwarf, **5:** 37
   red giant, **1:** 31; **5:** 24; **6:** 23
   scintillation, **6:** 13
   Sirius, **7:** 50
   study of, **7:** 16–17
   systems, **7:** 14–15, 50
   temperature, **6:** 16
   trails, **7:** *6*
   variable, **6:** 15, 23
   white dwarf, **1:** 31; **6:** 23, 25; **12:** 43
Star Wars program, **12:** 47
Sun, **1:** 27–36; **6:** *8;* **7:** 10. *See also* Solar
   color, **6:** 15
   composition, **1:** 30–31
   corona, **1:** *29, 34–35*

energy production, **1:** 9, 28
gravity on, **1:** 6, 8–9, 14
layers, **1:** 29–31; **6:** 10
mass, **1:** 10, 27
observing, **11:** 18, 22, 25
size of, **7:** 15
sunspots on, **1:** 32
surface, **1:** 6, *27*
temperature, **1:** 32; **6:** 8
Supernova, **5:** 15, 28; **6:** 25–26, 37; **11:** 34
Surveyor spacecraft, **8:** 32
Swigert, John, **2:** *48;* **8:** 43

T

Taurus, **6:** 26
Telescopes, **7:** 8, *14,* 22, *23;* **10:** 11; **12:** 25
   aerial, **7:** *7*
   anatomy of, **7:** 26–28
   Cassegrain, **7:** *26, 32,* 33
   coudé focus, **7:** *32,* 33
   early, **7:** 14
   Hooker, **7:** 25
   Hubble Space Telescope, **1:** 8, 26; **4:** 7; **6:** 41; **7:** 18, *24,* 37–44, 47; **9:** 44–47; **12:** *39–40,* 41, 49
   infrared, **6:** 27
   New Technology Telescope, **7:** 33
   Newtonian, **7:** 30, *31,–32*
   optical, **7:** 18, 26–33
   prime focus, **7:** 30, *32*
   radio, **6:** 13, 27, 40, 44, 46; **7:** *18,* 34–36
   reflecting, **5:** *19;* **7:** 26, *28, 30,* 37
   refracting, **7:** 25, 26, *28*
   solar, **11:** *21,* 25
   Uhuru, **12:** 43
   ultraviolet, **11:** 33; **12:** 42
   Very Large Array (New Mexico), **7:** 35–36; **12:** *13*
   X-ray, **6:** 27; **11:** 33
Telstar satellite, **12:** 32
Tereshkova, Valentina, **8:** 25; **10:** *13, 18*
Theory of relativity, **1:** 28; **7:** 20; **12:** 21
Thornton, Kathryn, **10:** *43*
Titan-Centaur rockets, **8:** *50*
Titan rockets, **2:** 44; **8:** 17
Titov, Gherman, **10:** 11, *13*
Tombaugh, Clyde, **4:** 49, 52–53
Truly, Richard, **9:** *36*

U

UFOs, **6:** 48
Ulysses spacecraft, **9:** 49; **12:** 44, *45,* 46
Universe
   age of, **7:** 44
   closed, **6:** 49
   end of, **6:** 48–49
   flat, **6:** 49
   geocentric view, **1:** 12; **5:** 13–14; **7:** 10, 12
   heliocentric view, **3:** 10; **5:** 14–15, 17, *18;* **7:** 13–15
   open, **6:** 49
   size of, **7:** 15, 44
   structure of, **7:** 20
Uranus, **1:** 14; **4:** 6, 40–44; **7:** 12, 39, 50
   atmosphere, **1:** 24; **4:** 41–42
   color, **1:** *24*
   composition, **4:** 41–42
   missions to, **4:** 13–14; **8:** 51–52; **12:** 8, 52
   moons, **4:** 8, *43–44*
   observing, **4:** 10–11
   orbit, **1:** 25
   period, **4:** 8
   ring system, **1:** 23; **4:** *42*
   rotation, **1:** 24; **4:** 8
   terrain, **3:** 19
Usachev, Yuri, **11:** *27, 35,* 39

V

Vacuums, **8:** 16; **11:** 18
Van Allen, James, **8:** 21
Van Allen belt, **8:** 23
Vanguard satellites, **8:** 22–23
Vega, **6:** *12*
Vega spacecraft, **3:** 31
Vela, **11:** 33
Velocity, **8:** 11
Venera spacecraft, **3:** 27, 31
VentureStar, **9:** 53
Venus, **1:** 14, *17;* **3:** 25–31; **7:** 50
   atmosphere, **1:** 17; **3:** 9, 14, *25,* 27
   diameter, **3:** 26
   distance to, **3:** 26
   gravity on, **3:** 19
   magnetic field, **3:** 30
   maps of, **3:** *28*
   missions to, **3:** 12; **8:** 48–50; **12:** 50
   observing, **3:** 9–11, 14
   rotation, **3:** 26
   size, **3:** 25
   storms on, **3:** 27
   temperature, **1:** 17; **3:** 27
   terrain, **1:** *18;* **3:** 6, 19, 28–30
   volcanoes on, **3:** *20,* 26, *29, 30, 31*
Viking spacecraft, **1:** 20; **3:** 16, 18, 46–47, 49; **8:** 49, *50*
von Braun, Wernher, **11:** *11*
Voskhod spacecraft, **8:** *31*
Voss, Janice, **10:** *50*
Vostok spacecraft, **8:** 23, *24–25, 29–30, 31;* **10:** 11
Voyager spacecraft, **4:** 13–14, 18, 20, 22, 30, 37, 42, 47–48; **6:** 18; **7:** 40, 51; **8:** 12, *13,* 51; **12:** 8, 46, *53*

W

Waves. *See* Rays and waves
Weightlessness, **8:** 7–8, 28; **10:** 20, 26–30; **11:** 11, 34, 49; **12:** 11
Weitz, Paul, **11:** *7, 20, 23*
White, Edward H., **8:** 34, *35;* **10:** *11*
Wide-Field Planetary Camera, **9:** 47–48; **12:** 41

X

X-Ray Multi-Mirror Mission (XMM), **12:** 43
X-Ray Timing Explorer (XTE), **12:** 43

Y

Young, John, **2:** 46, 49; **9:** *32*

Z

Zodiac, **5:** 32; **7:** 10
Zond spacecraft, **8:** 32

SET INDEX